LIGHT OF ALL LIFE

Dennis Knight

LIGHT
OF
ALL LIFE

THOUGHTS TOWARDS A PHILOSOPHY OF LIFE

RAYNOR C. JOHNSON

Dedicated to my
BELOVED MASTER
in
WHOSE LIGHT
is the experience of all life

PILGRIMS BOOK SERVICES
TASBURGH NORWICH ENGLAND

The author acknowledges with thanks permission to use
the extract from J. B. Priestley's *Rain upon Godshill*
published by William Heinemann Ltd on page 105, and
from R. H. Ward's *A Drug-Taker's Notes* published by
Victor Gollancz Ltd on page 113.

First published in the United Kingdom
April 1984 by permission of
Human Dimensions Publications,
Columbus, North Carolina, U.S.A.

ISBN: 0 946259 07 0

Photoset by Waveney Typesetters, Norwich
and printed by The Thetford Press Ltd., Thetford, Norfolk

Contents

Foreword

Dr Raynor Johnson's journeyings through the intellectual world over many years have taken an unusual course, but one very significant for today's world. For much of his life, as a physicist and spectroscopist, his work lay in the academic world, and it was as a scientist that he wrote a short book on psychical research. From then on, he began to write more from philosophical considerations and, as is clearly demonstrated in his pioneer book *The Imprisoned Splendour*, his path took him steadily towards the mystical insights which have led him to write *from* the whole man and *for* the whole man. This vision, combined with a habitual and beautiful serenity of mind, forms the hallmark of his style; and clearly the style is the man himself.

Subsequent writing steadily faced the classical problems of human existence, as they appear to modern man incarnated in a universe of mystery, in terms of philosophy, religion or pioneering human experience.

In *Light of All Life* he reaches the summit of his quest, where the crown of life is seen as the willing surrender to a meaning beyond any the intellect can work out for itself, but which, when experienced by the whole man, then finds a willing acquiescence in the intellect too. The book is largely concerned – and has to be concerned – with those weighty and so insoluble-seeming problems at that mysterious point where life itself meets us with its own meanings, where, in Wordsworth's famous words

> The heavy and the weary weight
> Of all this unintelligible world
> Is lightened . . . and . . .
> We see into the life of things.

Dr Johnson points a way, but leaves each reader free to take it, in whole or in part. It is a way which over his forty years of search points to a still distant destination. We can choose to make our own way towards it at our pace, but it is also making its own way towards us. That is the other half of the adventure; the meaning and significance in life which, like the Hound of Heaven, is pursuing us, whatever direction we choose to turn. Then it is that experiences come about — the book narrates a number drawn from separate testimonies — where the hidden sides of life have suddenly revealed themselves, and shown a vision which afterwards can never be gainsaid.

I can only conclude by saying once more, as I did as the privileged chairman when the lectures which make up this book were first given in London's College of Psychic Studies, 'The man is as fine as his writing.' Each indeed rings true to the other.

Paul Beard

Reincarnation: The Wheel of Births and Deaths

Few people do any serious thinking outside a small personal area of their special interests. They would no more think of doing so than a pious Christian would study Islam or Buddhism, or a sceptical scientist would study psychical research. The great majority have conditioned minds: they have been moulded by the persistent power of suggestion (to which we are all gullible when young). In later life these powers of suggestion are sometimes called advertisement, sometimes scientific authority, sometimes religious authority: whatever name they are known by, they convey to people the idea that they are necessarily right.

When I first started to think seriously – in my late thirties – about life and death and destiny, the orthodox Christian belief that souls which appear on earth in physical bodies are created fresh from the hands of God and come here with one life to live, seemed to me naive, childish and most improbable. The quality of this life was supposed to determine their everlasting future of bliss or torment. Little if anything was apparently known about what lay outside this physical existence – before birth or after death.

I found the ideas of reincarnation and karma have always had a place in the religious teaching of Hinduism and Buddhism, where they have been regarded as fundamental to any understanding of life. In simple terms the concept is that there is a centre of individual consciousness which is immortal (we may call it the 'soul') and this makes a series of contacts with the physical world, creating physical bodies to do so. It is reasonable to suppose that what the soul has done once it can do again and again, in the interests of its own

1

growth and development. Each time it builds a new personality perhaps in quite a different environment and period of history, and it distils after death from each of these transient personalities some wisdom and experience which it stores within itself.

Some people are convinced of the truth of this idea because they have recalled memories of former lives. Others have been convinced by the testimony of those who have, and by the light which has been thrown upon the puzzles and problems of their life. Let us approach the subject by looking first at some of the mysteries of life.

If the bodies of babies born into the world are vehicles of newly-created souls who are beginning their first and only incarnate life, why are some of them so badly handicapped from the start? At a defenceless stage some of them are subject to cruelty, neglect or callousness which physically or psychologically warps them from the start. Other babies are given wonderful opportunities and many gifts, including the boon of loving and understanding parents. It is obvious that babies cannot embody newly-created souls without imputing favouritism or callous indifference to their Creator. This is unthinkable. If, however, we assume that all souls have made a long journey through time in many lives, and that each further incarnation is determined in its conditions by the self-created karma of these past lives, we approach this problem quite differently.

It would be unfair to judge a play on the basis of one brief glimpse of a scene on the stage. We would require to know what went before that scene, and what was coming after, if we were to talk of the justice or fairness of the play.

The blessings and hardships upon which the new-born child enters may have been all self-created if we could see them in terms of the past lives of the soul. This outlook then permits us to believe in a principle of justice and love running through the created world. The things that stagger us can be seen as the working out of just law, from this wider standpoint.

2

A particular case of the problem of inequality occurs in the appearance of genius at an early age. Chopin and Mozart, to take the examples of two musicians, showed musical maturity at a very youthful age, and they composed and executed compositions with a maturity which could not be explained if this was their first appearance on earth. Sir William Hamilton at the age of five could answer a difficult mathematical question, and would then run off to play with his toy cart and horses.

If we accept that each soul may have had many lives in the past, and gathered great facility in these fields, our only problem is the rather unusual overflow of this knowledge into the life of which we are talking. Sometimes the marks of genius fade out, perhaps in the early teens, as though the soul, as soon as it was able to do so, threw up other fields of interest and withdrew the special one in the interest of a more balanced development. The puzzle of the prodigy at an early age cannot be ignored because it is rare.

Most people have commented that sometimes in one and the same family, born of the same two parents, and subject to the same external influences, its members may show most striking differences in disposition, interests, sensitivity, outlook, intellect, etc. If we recognise that each child is the expression of a soul which has had many lives and many interests through a long past, it is not surprising that these differences and contrasts show up.

Although love at first sight and hate at first sight are frequently exploited by romantic novelists, they correspond to not uncommon experiences in life. We have at least a plausible explanation if it is recognised that we may be dealing with emotional reactions and relationships which have pre-existed this life. My wife and I knew a couple of considerable culture and intelligence, who met and married in middle-life. At their first meeting the woman knew that the man she was meeting was the same person who had been her husband in a former life in another country in a very different setting. Indeed many years before they met, the lady had a vision of a fragment of this former life, which came back to

3

her with all the force of a poignant memory. Until the moment of meeting in this life, she had no male acquaintance with which she could associate this visionary glimpse. Afterwards she had no doubt whatever.

The claim is often made for the soul that it is potentially immortal. By this is meant that its nature is eternal and rooted outside time, although it may manifest itself in time. If, as is commonly said, the soul has an infinite future stretching ahead of it, why should it be thought unreasonable that an infinite past lies behind it? Indeed, to be rooted in eternity presupposes this.

These are a few of the puzzles of human life, and many more can be mentioned. If we accept the soul's pre-existence in prior lives we have a viewpoint from which they may perhaps be resolved.

The idea of a plurality of lives is a very ancient one. It belongs to a very long tradition in Indian thought. Krishna, the great enlightened sage, who teaches his disciple Arjuna in the *Bhagavad Gita* says to him on one occasion: 'I have been born again and again, from time to time: thou too, O Arjuna. My births are known to me, but thou knowest not thine.'

Reincarnation was part of the teachings of the Mystery Schools in ancient Greece and Egypt, It was an idea that was talked about by the Jewish people at the time Jesus was preaching in Palestine. You may recall that when Jesus had healed a man blind from birth, he was asked the question, 'Master, who did sin, this man, or his parents, that he should be born blind?' Obviously, if he was *born* blind, the circumstances of his sinning must have been in a former life. On another occasion Jesus had asked His disciples, 'Whom do men say that I am?' and received the answer, 'John the Baptist: but some say Elias; and others, One of the prophets.'

Jesus did not deny or confirm the popular notion that a person then alive could be the reincarnation of a great figure in the past. On another occasion He heard His disciples discussing the idea that before the expected Messiah of the

Jews should come, Elijah must first appear. He intervened in their conversation to say 'Elias is come already, and they knew him not, but have done unto him whatsoever they listed.' The record says that then the disciples realised He was speaking to them about John the Baptist. The episode is described twice by St Matthew, in the 11th and in the 17th chapters of his gospel.

It may be remarked however that Jesus did not apparently teach the theme of reincarnation, and surely it was an important idea? I think two things should be said in reply. The first is that there are many important themes which apparently Jesus did not teach to the multitude, such as survival of death, or the pressing problems of pain and suffering, time and evil. The teachings of Jesus, as recorded in the Gospels, are essentially practical, not metaphysical. His words to the multitudes who listened were to show them how to live the good life in a difficult age, to show them how much God loved them, and what He expected from them, and how they ought to love each other. There are good grounds however for believing that both Jesus and John the Baptist had close links with the Mystery School of the Essenes, and the truths of reincarnation and karma were part of their tradition. Mark records that, while to the multitudes He taught in parables, privately to His inner circle of disciples He taught and explained many other things.

We shall now consider the positive evidence in support of reincarnation. First, there is a steadily growing amount of evidence that some individuals recall fragments of past lives. If there were no memories interlinking lives, conveying to some individuals the subjective certainty that they were memories, reincarnation would be no more than an interesting hypothesis. If the question is asked 'How do you know that these are memories and not phantasies?' it is sufficient to say that they may convey knowledge that has not been acquired in this life, but which investigation shows subsequently to be correct. In addition to memories from former lives there are sometimes peculiar emotional reactions carried

5

over, peculiar physical characteristics, and special skills or abilities. We shall look at some examples of all these.

In his book *My Land and My People* His Holiness the Dalai Lama describes the procedure which took place when he was selected to his office. It is believed that these procedures ensure that the same soul succeeds to this high office.

Following directions given by the 13th Dalai Lama before he died indicating the district in which he expected to be reborn, a committee was set up to make a search, and they found a 3-year-old boy who appeared to fulfil the conditions. The committee brought with them two identical black rosaries, one of which had belonged to the 13th Dalai Lama. When they offered these to the boy he chose the one which was his and put it round his neck. A similar test was completed successfully with yellow rosaries. Then they offered him two drums, a very small one used for calling attendants, and an ornate attractive drum with golden straps. He chose the former and began to beat it in the way which is customary during prayers. Finally they presented two walking sticks. The boy touched the first one and looked at it with hesitation, then he took the other and held it firmly in his hand. The hesitation had arisen through an interesting fact — that the former Dalai Lama had originally used the first walking stick, but had subsequently given it to another Lama.

In his fascinating book *The Way of the White Clouds* Lama Govinda, its author, has a section on reincarnation in which he says 'For myself, rebirth is neither a theory nor a belief, but an experience.' The full account of his own personal evidence should be read in full, but here is a short synopsis.

As a young man aged 21 he had been residing in the island of Capri. On one occasion he attended a spiritualistic seance in which, by a table tilting technique, answers were being given to questions about the former lives of persons sitting around the table. For the young Govinda a name, apparently Latin, was mentioned, but none was familiar with it. Some time later, Govinda was reading to a learned older friend a

6

story, which he had written in his boyhood, which he describes as part of a mystic novel 'in which my religious convictions and religious experiences were symbolically expressed'. His older friend suddenly said, 'Where did you get this from?' and went on to mention the same name as had been spoken in the seance, saying that the story, the images and the ideas were all similar although they had been written by this other author a century ago.

Govinda naturally decided to order the books of this writer, but they could not be traced in the Italian bookshops. Before he finally got hold of these books, Govinda attended by invitation, a party in Capri, which was being given in honour of a visiting German scholar. Govinda was introduced to him, and noticed that the visitor was not only taken a little aback when introduced, but frequently looked across at him during the course of the evening. When Govinda later met his hostess, he inquired about this German scholar. She told Govinda that he had been amazed at the likeness of Govinda's face to the only known portrait of a German mystic-poet whose biography he was at present writing and who had lived about a century ago. When the books ordered came finally to hand Lama Govinda not only recognised parts of the story as similar to his own, but found some passages almost identical with his boyhood essay. Still more impressive was the fact that the underlying theme and ideals which he had expressed in his essay had been there a century ago in the life of this writer.

Lama Govinda concludes this amazing story by reflecting, 'It is not my idea to be reborn for ever in this world: but neither do I believe we can abandon it until we have fulfilled our task in it.'

The work of Dr Ian Stevenson, a medical Professor at an American university may appropriately be mentioned here. He published a book in 1966 entitled, *Twenty Cases Suggestive of Reincarnation*. One of these cases is mentioned in some detail in Lama Govinda's book just referred to. It is the case of a little girl of 3 called Shanta Devi, who was born in

7

1926 and lived at Delhi with her parents. She started to talk of her husband (Kedarnath Chaubey) and her son who lived in Muttra, a town about 100 miles distant from Delhi. When the girl was about 8, her great-uncle began to feel that her many statements merited serious investigation. He therefore visited Muttra himself and corroborated many things which the girl had said. Later on, an unannounced visit was made to Delhi by the husband and his son, and the girl identified them at once.

A local committee of Muttra was formed to witness the reactions of the girl when she paid her first visit to Muttra in this life. Dr Stevenson says that she made at least twenty-four statements which were memories of her former life, established as correct, and she made no incorrect statements. Clearly the relatively short interval between her death in Muttra (in childbirth), and her birth in Delhi greatly facilitated verification. Lama Govinda states that she has not married again in this life, but that she possesses a dedicated religious outlook and is a well-qualified school-teacher.

Dr Stevenson cautiously concludes in his book, 'The evidence which I have assembled and reviewed here . . . does justify I believe a much more extensive and sympathetic study of the hypothesis than it has hitherto received in the West. Further investigation of apparent memories of former incarnations may well establish reincarnation as the most probable explanation of these experiences.'

I will present to you one other example of memories carried over from a former life and recalled in a series of dreams. The lady who sent me this case was a distinguished historian, but she has now died. The story is her own life-story and I have no doubt of its validity.

To what extent dreams are true could be endlessly disputed; but when I was about eleven years old, I had a series of dreams concerning which I kept silence, as I had been told it was very wrong to boast. As in the dreams I had manifestly been of some consequence. I thought it would be wrong to claim this, as I was of no account today.

The dream was of being a prisoner in a place which I knew to be the Tower of London. I had not seen it in real life, but I had no doubt where I was. It was very cold weather although in waking life, a hot summer. I was aware that I had been condemned to death, and I hoped that the execution would not be on so cold a day, because to shiver would look like fear, and would be most un-dignified! I was not at all apologetic, or inclined to admit that I had been in the wrong; nor was I tired of life. I felt sorry to have my activities cut short; but consoled myself with the assumption of a clear conscience. This, I used to dream over and over again, and after being in the dream a vigorous man, to wake up and be a little girl felt rather strange.

At last the dream changed, and I was standing on a scaffold which must have been newly erected as it smelt of sawdust. Everything was decorous and decent. The executioner knelt and apologised for what he was about to do. I took the axe from his hand and felt it, and handed it back bidding him to do his duty. Someone (Sir George Trevelyan, I think), alleges that beheading was painless. How can he know? On the contrary, it was excruciating. But now comes the part of the dream which most impressed me. The executioner was holding up my head and pronouncing some usual formula, but I, my real self, was looking on — feeling extraordinarily free from all my woes, and much more vigorous than previously. I must have believed firmly in the immortality of the soul, and yet I was utterly astonished to find myself in the dream so much more vividly alive than previously.

When I woke up, I made a drawing of the axe, which was of a peculiar shape. Some years after this, I asked to be taken to the Tower of London, and I explained to a friendly gunsmith that I wanted to write a history, but could not understand the battles perfectly until I understood the weapons.

'Right you are, Missy,' he said, and demonstrated to me

the various uses of pike, lance, crossbow, etc. I then asked, had he an axe that beheaded people? He said, 'Yes, this certainly beheaded the Jacobite Lords, but it is supposed to be very much older.' Somehow, I was not surprised that it proved to be the very shape of the axe in my dream. I said, 'May I hold it in my hand for a moment, please,' for I felt that if I touched it I should never have the execution dream again. I took off my glove, felt the edge, and then handed it back again.

My aunt who was with me, made no comment, but long afterwards when reading the typescript of my book, especially of the treason trials, she said, 'I did not make any remark at the time, but do you remember asking to see the axe in the Tower? It seemed odd for a gentle girl to be interested in the method of execution, but you looked almost exultant when you handed it back to the gunsmith, and he gave me such a look as much to say, "How incongruous".' I have resolutely not tried to imagine who I might have been in the past − but long before I heard the word 'reincarnation', I felt convinced that I had lived in some of the periods I wanted to write about; also that I had come back for a purpose.

An old peasant woman, a seventh child of a seventh child, said to me − and she did not know who I was, 'You do need rest; but yer wont never 'ev it; and if yer died termorrer, yer'd come 'urrying back because yer work aint finished yet'. She was a fisherman's wife, old and frail and quite illiterate. But she apparently 'saw' various people out of the past. 'One of the gentlemen was you, me dear,' she said, 'and couldn't you handle a sword in those days!'

The lady whose account I have just presented, also related to me the following:

About 1913 my cousin and I had occasion to examine some illustrated Persian manuscripts. A few days later, a neighbour asked if she could bring to tea a French friend who would be interested to see an old English country house. To our surprise Mlle de H. did not look French, but she reminded us both of one of the Persian medieval paintings. She had none of the vivacity of a French woman but a courteous aloofness. When we got to know her better she told us something about herself.

She had been an only child, and very lonely; so she had, as her parents supposed, invented a baby language in which she sang little songs to herself, and recited what she called poems, which they regarded as sheer gibberish.

Her father had a cousin, a Jesuit priest, whom he had not seen since before this child was born. The priest's career had been set in the East, but on his return to France he came to visit his kinsfolk and spent some days with them. The child, then about five, grew weary of listening to grown-up conversations and sitting in a corner began to murmur to herself her usual recitations. The priest stopped talking and listened, and then asked 'Where did Laurence learn Persian?'

'Persian,' said her father, 'it's nonsense, sound without sense.' The priest then asked her to speak to him in her own language – which she did – and then he said to her father, 'This is Persian, not Persian of today, but of the epic era.' The parents were amazed: they said nobody who knew Persian had been near the child or near them. They could not account for her conduct. They had none but European heredity, etc. After he left they forbad her to talk her gibberish any more.

She told us later that she had never felt as though she really 'belonged' to France, but she had deliberately not pursued the Persian line of enquiry, as she had come to the conclusion for some reason unknown, she was meant to be taken away from it. She had however no doubt that France was not her real country. Nor was she attracted to modern Persia. Her Persian recitations, the meaning of which she had not known, were of the days of 'ride and shoot and speak the truth' of Persian epic poetry.

Such experiences as these, and others of which it would be

11

possible to write, point to the likelihood that as personalities we are transient expressions of a deeper underlying self or soul, and that these souls are engaged on an enterprise of unfolding and development which involves many experiences over very long stretches of time. We have remarked already on child-prodigies, who at an early age exhibit skills or knowledge that could not possibly have been acquired in the first few years of childhood. Musicians such as Mozart and Chopin are good examples, and we have a possible explanation if we can postulate that in former lives these abilities were very highly developed. In rare cases there seems to be a freakish overflow into the present life. Note that in the Persian case, the child did not know the meaning of the poetry she recited.

We have already cited the remarkable resemblance between Lama Govinda and a minor mystical poet, which evidently impressed the visiting German scholar although he knew nothing of any connection through reincarnation. In some of Dr Stevenson's cases children were found to carry birthmarks or show behaviour patterns corresponding to the mode of death in the last life. An experienced chiropracter told me that he had learned to recognize certain vertebral changes that he associated with hanging in a previous life, and others which he associated with beheading. If memory preserves highly traumatic factors it is conceivable that they may persist, and modify the etheric blueprint upon which the physical material is precipitated for life after life.

It is not uncommon to find that people have phobias, such as of being buried alive, of going near to the edge of a cliff, of diving into deep cold water, etc., where no known cause can be unearthed in this life. In some cases it has been possible to find the traumatic incident which gave rise to it in an earlier life, and then the phobia has cleared up.

Philippa Torrens records that she was told by a medium, 'You had a brother in this life, who passed over in the war. You have been brother and sister many times. I see you as the children of a Roman official, living on the south bank of the Thames estuary. One moonlight night, when your brother was about 16, he went out on the river in a rowing boat, fishing, and he was drowned.' The writer continues. 'My mind flew back to a strange incident in this, the only life I know . . . moonlight on the lake, my brothers, cousins, and myself in warm deep water playing a version of an unlovely game called "Murder". Two grown-ups were there in a big rowing boat to see that nobody drowned. And I remember how quite suddenly my brother lost his nerve and began to struggle out of the water and into the boat . . . It could not have been more out of character. My brother was the bravest of the brave as his subsequent career showed. He could swim like a fish, and I never knew him to show perturbation, much less panic, in his life – save that once. Was it an echo from another life, very long ago, evoked by the moon, the water, the boat and the game?'

In his book *The Cathars and Reincarnation* Dr Arthur Guirdham presents a lot of interesting material which is plausible from the viewpoint of reincarnation. The Cathars were a sect who suffered greatly from persecution in the Wars of Religion, and in the Middle Ages. Many persons in the vicinity appeared to come as patients to Dr Guirdham who remarked how many of them had recurrent nightmares or dreams going back to the times of persecution. He mentions one patient who had distressing years'-long symptoms and a recurrent nightmare connected with an event occurring on 28th May 1242. After an encounter with another individual the distress and the nightmare cleared up within a few days. The occasioning incident 700 years before had been brought to the surface and faced. Dr Guirdham makes the interesting and significant statement, 'My approach to reincarnation was not deliberate or logical. I was not even willing. It was forced on me: and I marvel that during so many years I resisted enlightenment.'

I will mention an episode that came under my personal notice some years ago. A middle-aged lady, whom I knew slightly already, came to see me. She had held a very responsible position in a large organisation but had retired from it believing that this course was the right one. The standards of

13

professional work, which she believed should be preserved, were steadily falling, and all her efforts to preserve them were being frustrated by another person. She found herself becoming very depressed and started to think in terms of hanging herself. At this juncture a friend, whom she had known well many years earlier, came over from the U.S.A. and renewed the old link. This friend had a well developed psychic faculty and one day said to her, 'I think if we were quiet now, I could tell you something of your past life.'

In that life it appeared that she had suffered a great deal and in despair had hung herself while quite young. She had been permitted to come back to Earth after some ten years, in order to expiate her fault. This she had done by her devotion to her profession and self-sacrifice. She was now free to retire from her position with a clear conscience, and another job in which she would find satisfaction was awaiting her if she wanted it. There was much more detail into which it is unnecessary to enter. It is sufficient to say that this disclosure of the soul's past placed the events of the present in a new light and carried conviction to her. Her depression lifted; her confidence returned, and she took the new position with a conviction that she had done the work which she had returned to do.

Having presented illustrations and evidence in support of reincarnation it is opportune to consider a number of objections to the idea which are often expressed. One of the questions asked is 'Why do not people, in general, remember their past lives?' A few, as we have seen, do recall fragments. One reply would be, 'Why should we expect them to?' We know that memory normally becomes very poor as we approach our earliest years and birth: why then should we expect to recall memories still more remote? I think we should realise too that forgetting may play as useful a function as remembering.

A learned or skilled person does not need to recall every detail of the laborious way he has come — perhaps all the efforts he made as a schoolboy and the practice he had, and the problems he tried in vain to solve. Mercifully these are forgotten, but what he retains is the experience and the principles. With these in his memory he can tackle any new problem which is presented to him. So it is in life where we are faced with new situations and opportunities. We have available to us as intuition the experience and prompting of the soul based upon its past lives.

Another question – 'Is reincarnation voluntary or is it inevitable?' Generally speaking, I think it is inevitable except in the case of rare souls who have come down from the Kingdom to help mankind, or for those few souls who under a Master's guidance earn on Earth the qualifications which will allow them after death to climb through those levels of consciousness up to the Kingdom – a level of no normal return. As we shall see in the next chapter, the ideas of reincarnation and karma are really inseparable, for on this earth level in the midst of the Opposites, unless we are under a Master's guidance we shall almost inevitably build up more karma – both 'good' and 'bad' – while we are discharging other karma. It is this karma – and the vain hope of discharging one's accounts with earth – which brings souls back again and again to the physical level.

And another, 'Does rebirth include the possibility of descent below the human level into say, an animal body?' This is possible, although, I understand, not commonplace. Where however, there has been great cruelty to others, especially to animals, the experience of suffering in the form of an animal may be the best, perhaps the only way of reforming the individual. We must recognise that there is a law of complete justice running through the world. It is not punitive but intended to be redemptive.

I think I have never talked on the subject of reincarnation without someone raising with me the relationship between reincarnation and the population explosion which it is said, will double the earth's numbers by the end of this century. It is quite clear that no one has knowledge on which to base any views. If the number of souls associated with the human race is constant then movements of such souls both ways between the astral and higher levels on the one hand, and the physical level on the other, must affect the physical population. If the creation of souls is still taking place then the numbers of souls seeking physical embodiment would be expected to increase. All one can say is that from time to time in history there may be periods when earth conditions are favourable for the discharge of a great deal of karma by souls on higher levels – and this present period may be one of them.

Still another objection to reincarnation is that it is unjust. The conditions of the present life are all karmic, i.e., they derive from the thoughts, words, and deeds, of a personality who lived perhaps a century or two ago. Are these two personalities not distinct, and is it right and just that the present one should be suffering or enjoying the karma of the earlier one? To this the answer must be that all questions of justice are to be referred to the soul of which the two personalities are temporary expressions.

It is the growth and unfoldment of the soul which is important, and it is for this end that incarnation is undertaken. If we walked across a theatre and went out again at the opposite door, we would glimpse on the stage things which might be very misleading, or lead to very faulty judgement. We should need to know what went before and what was coming after, before we could express an opinion; before we could talk of justice.

This in outline is the case for reincarnation and it has had a long history. It has always had a fundamental place in Hinduism and Buddhism, and among the Greeks it was taught by Empedocles, Pythagoras, and Plato. Some of the early Christian Church Fathers accepted it, but then in A.D. 551 the Church decided it was a heresy. The Druids taught this doctrine in Gaul. Many philosophers and poets have been attracted by it and John Masefield wrote:

> I hold that when a person dies
> His soul returns again to earth;
> Arrayed in some new flesh-disguise,
> Another mother gives him birth.
> With sturdier limbs and brighter brain
> The old soul takes the road again.

Shelley, Wordsworth, Tennyson, Browning, Rossetti, Long-fellow and Whitman could be quoted in support. AE the Irish mystic and poet writes in his book *Song and Its Fountains*:

> 'Looking back on the past I have vivid sense of a being seeking incarnation here, beginning with those first faint intuitions of beauty, and those early dreamings which were its forerunners. It was no angelic thing, pure and new from a foundry of souls, which sought embodiment, but a being stained with the dust and travel of a long travel through time, carrying with it unsated desires base and august, and as I divined of it, myriads of memories and a secret wisdom. It was not simple but infinitely complex as a being must be which has been in many worlds and all it has experienced has become part of it . . . It was a being avidly desirous of life, while another part was cold to this, but was endlessly seeking for the spirit.'

For my own part, and having had some fragmentary glimpses of former lives – of which I have no wish to write – I have no doubt at all that this law of reincarnation is basic to our development and that it is only from this standpoint that we can unravel many of the mysteries which surround our mortal life.

I am aware that some people react rather emotionally against the idea of reincarnation, and I have found two reasons why this is commonly the case. Sometimes a person has had a disturbing and sad or tumultuous life in which they have had to meet many hard blows. They react naturally against even the possibility that other lives are to come, in which the same hardships or others may have once more to be suffered or contended with. Of course this assumption has no basis. There would be no point whatever in meeting like situations again any more than one would send back a schoolboy into a class to repeat the work he had already done the previous year.

Some people dislike the thought that the possiblity of

17

reincarnation of a beloved friend before they themselves pass over at death may prevent their being reunited. This is quite an unlikely possibility. While it is theoretically possible the time which most souls spend on the astral planes is likely to be many years – perhaps indeed centuries. Myers, in one of his communications through Geraldine Cummins, has written these comforting words:

> 'Death seems terrible to the average man because of its apparent loneliness. If he but knew it, his fears are vain; his dread of being reft from the Pattern – that it to say from those he loves – has no foundation, has no real substance behind it. For wherever he may journey after death, always will he be caught again into the design of which he is a part, always will he find again, however deep his temporary oblivion or however varied his experience, certain human souls who were knit into his earth-life, who were loved deeply, if sometimes blindly or evilly, by him in those bygone days.'

I shall discuss at length in the next chapter the law of Karma which is intimately connected with the law of Reincarnation. The two are interwoven and are the twin pillars on which can be built an understanding of life as we live it.

Karma: the Law of Cause and Effect

In our Western world we are all familiar with the law of cause and effect. If certain things concur, then certain other things always happen. The first group is called the cause of the second happening, and the latter is called the effect of the first. The observations of scientists have been largely directed to linking things together in such chains of cause and effect. It is analysis of these kinds of data which has led to Natural Law. All this is familiar to everyone: the physical world is ruled by Law. When we come to consider Man himself, who, in the simplest terms must be considered a synthesis of body, mind and soul, we seem to be uncertain of the rule of law on these higher levels of ourselves. Some people talk as though these higher levels were the domain of caprice or chance: this is nonsense, for the Law of cause and effect runs through all levels on which time operates. It is called in the Eastern philosophies the law of *Karma*, and it amounts to this: so far as human beings are concerned there is no such things as chance or accident, but everything that happens to them fits into the pattern of cause and effect. Each living person at some time has set going his own pattern of causation and is meeting the consequences.

We can all start off from agreed ground. Each of us came into this life; we were born to particular parents, of a particular nationality, at a particular point in history. Suppose we had been born to Esquimaux, or Arabian, or African parents, how different would have been our physique, our education, our cultural interests, our dreams and opportunities. Instead of being born when we were, we might have been born 100 or perhaps 1,000 years ago. How different our outlook would have been: would we have been the same persons? The existing facts are what they are: but what are their causes? With innumerable other possibilities, why did these particular ones come to fruition?

Or look back over your *present* life and reflect that at innumerable points other paths could have been taken. It looks as though the way we took was determined sometimes by the 'merest accident'. Perhaps we appear to have been influenced by a headache, a missed train, a shower of rain, or a casual word. If we reject the conception that we are playthings of chance, the sport of destiny, or feathers blown on the wind of change, we must accept the operation of a law of cause and effect and ask ourselves the pertinent question, 'What were the causes which led us to take the way that in fact we did take?' I put to you one of the most important questions about life: 'How far are we free?' Is there such a thing as chance or accident in relation to the souls of men?' If we do not make up our minds about this issue, how can we have any satisfying philosophy of life?

I ask you to look a little longer at the facts of familiar life. There are some people who seem to have been always the favourites of fortune. From earliest childhood they were blest with kind parents and many good friends. They have had good minds and healthy bodies, an encouraging environment, and the open door of opportunity. For others the face of life appears to have been one long struggle against handicaps, suffering and tragedy. Such inequalities are strange and baffling if you are concerned that there should be a law of justice in this world.

Here is a young surgeon who has qualified himself, by ten or more years of hard study, to do some brilliant work: then suddenly he is stricken with blindness. Here is a young mother attacked by terminal cancer and her young family left orphans. Here is a youth who has been accidentally shot through the spine, and he must lie on his bed as a cripple for the rest of his life. A tile is lifted from a roof by a gust of wind and it falls on a child in a pram and damages his brain

20

for life. These are what we call tragedies and apparently no sort of vigilance or conduct on the part of the victim could have averted them. But *if* we are victims of chance or accident in this life, where does justice to the individual come in? If we are *not* victims of chance or accident, then what and where are the basic causes from which these effects resulted?

You may ask, 'What do you mean by chance or accident?' The answer is, 'A chance event is one to which so many different factors have contributed that no prediction or forecast could possibly be made of the consequences, so that no care or vigilance could have avoided it.' Indeed it is doubtful if there could be a world like ours in which the possibilities for both good and ill do not exist. Consider for example the tile which got blown from a roof and damaged a child's brain. One of the essential factors was a high wind which could be traced to temperature variations, and the physical laws which control air movement. These operate in the interests of the planet: and these 'chance' events so-called which have advantages for most of the time, may occasionally create misfortune at other times.

The more we think about it, the clearer it becomes that it is the problem of justice to the individual which is basic. If there is only one life to live – the one we know at present –and if there is no enduring soul, then no sense can be made of life. The teachings of the East – and I suggest of all the great Sages of both East and West – is that there are many lives to be lived. This is the doctrine of reincarnation which we have already talked about. Each life that we live is of a transient personality created or budded-off as it were, by the soul. The experience and wisdom gathered through it is withdrawn into the permanent enduring entity – the soul.

When a soul reincarnates it enters upon the new life with a little greater experience than hitherto, and its stored wisdom is available to the new personality as what we call 'intuition'. The question whether life is just to the individual must be referred to the soul and not to the individualised, transient personality. As I suggested in the last chapter, if we walked

21

across a theatre and saw something happening on the stage, but walked out of the opposite door, we should have no adequate grounds for making a judgement on the play through that glimpse. We should need to know what had preceded it and what would follow after. So it is with human life.

We must now consider more carefully the meaning of karma, which is always taught alongside the idea of reincarnation. It is in fact karma – as the law of cause and effect – which links our many lives together in a rational way. All that we have set going through our thoughts, words and deeds, has affected both ourselves and others. That which we have been responsible for creating we must answer for, sometime, somewhere. The law of karma will require us to meet these consequences, perhaps in the same life, perhaps in a future life. If there are debts, we must repay them; if there are dues, we must receive them. According to this law, no one gets away with anything. This law has been expressed in different forms. St Paul wrote, 'Whatsoever a man soweth, that shall he also reap.' Jesus said, 'Judge not, that ye be not judged: for with what judgement ye judge, ye shall be judged: and with what measure ye mete, it shall be measured to you again.'

With the twin laws of reincarnation and karma to guide us, we can begin to look at life from a truer and higher standpoint. Each successive birth and life is in circumstances created by the karma of our past lives. What superficially might be described as unfair or unjust is the result of our own creation. The karma we have set in motion is stored up on a high level of the mind, and this becomes the network linking different lives. When the time is ripe, the seeds of some of this past karma are allowed to fall into manifestation, and we are presented with opportunities to discharge our past debts, or set right things where we went astray before.

We should remember also that good, as well as ill, returns to us. Indeed, all that we may regard as the given-ness of life: place and time of birth, our parents and friends and enemies, our health, our abilities, our opportunities, our interests –

virtually, all that comes to us without our choice or effort is karmic. It is part of the great Pattern which we have ourselves been weaving so long as Time has been. All souls have in themselves an inherent knowledge about the conditions of life – although this knowledge seldom rises up to the consciousness of the ego. Buried perhaps beneath a lot of debris, the one hidden yearning of all souls is to return to their Creator, to the country of their origin.

Each time the soul undertakes incarnation it has a general preview of the conditions upon which it is entering and hopes that the life lived will result in some positive steps towards the goal. Whether it does so or not will depend largely upon the ego's reaction to the situations. The great majority of souls are only beginning to awaken, and they are virtually prisoners of the ego which rules the personality.

A Lebanese sage wrote about karma in these terms:

> 'Man invites his own calamities and then protests against the irksome guests, having forgotten how, and when, and where he penned and sent out the invitations. Time does not forget, and Time delivers in due season each invitation to the right address, and Time conducts each invitee to the dwelling of the host . . .
>
> 'Accept a misfortune as though it were a fortune. For a misfortune, once understood is soon transformed into a fortune; while a fortune misconstrued quickly becomes a misfortune. There are no accidents in Time and Space, but all things are ordered by the Omni-Will.'

I have heard the doctrine of karma criticised as being fatalistic. I take it that a fatalistic attitude is one in which a man says, 'It is my fate: I can do nothing about it.' Surely this is a misrepresentation of karma, for it teaches that we ourselves – in conjunction with others – have created our own karma. Moreover, by meeting it in the right spirit, we can cancel the debt and need face it no more. Also it teaches that we create the future by our present attitudes.

The same misrepresentation of karma could lead a man to

suppose that he is not his brother's keeper; that compassion and the helping hand extended to a brother are a waste of time. That every misfortune is 'his karma'. This is a complete travesty of the doctrine, for none of us live in isolation, and our links with others are part of our karmic pattern.

There is a story told of two men, who were both good swimmers, walking along the side of a river when a poor wretch, who could not swim, fell in and looked like drowning. One of the men proceeded quickly to throw off his coat and shoes preparatory to jumping in to help him. The other said however, 'Let him alone, it is his karma'. This was a foolish remark. It was the man's karma to fall into the river at a time when there were two good swimmers on the river-bank to help him. Furthermore, it might have been his karma to simply get his suit wet, rather than to be drowned!

Who are we to judge any situation? To say to a poor cripple 'Thus have you earned' would be a most presumptuous judgement. His karma will certainly have been linked with others and we do not know those links. Furthermore some great souls may choose to incarnate into conditions of hardship, handicap, and suffering, in order to help more effectively other souls they love. Furthermore the law of karma, while utterly just, is not mechanically rigid. Always something new is capable of entering in, whether it is our different reaction, the choices of others, or the descent of grace from higher beings as a result of prayer, etc. We are all rich with treasure we have not earned, but which others have earned for us. This is, of course, the happy side of karma, which we welcome!

To those who find the ideas of karma and reincarnation difficult to grasp I think it is helpful to read some book such as Gina Cerminara's *Many Mansions*. When Edgar Cayce was alive many people consulted him about their health, or peculiar problems, or life-situation. He had the remarkable faculty of reading some of the past lives of the patient, often showing the root cause, perhaps set going many centuries ago, of the present difficulties and problems. The book mentioned gives an account of many of these cases.

Another book which I found stimulating is H. K. Challoner's book *The Wheel of Rebirth*. Out of a long series of lives recovered by various methods and described in the book, there is an account of seven lives covering a period of some thousands of years, and lived in Atlantis, Egypt, Persia, Greece, Germany, Italy and England. The thread of karma is traced through them all and a particularly valuable aspect of this book is the comment made by a teacher, who is an advanced soul, showing how each of these lives followed karmically from the preceding one in which a right or wrong reaction had been made to the life-situation.

Another book well worth reading is called *Initiation* by Elizabeth Haitch – and there are others. Most persons who have been serious students of the evidence will have studied Dr Ian Stevenson's book *Twenty Cases Suggestive of Reincarnation* which was published many years ago by the American Society for Psychical Research. This book, together with the work he has done since then, present a very strong case to which he draws the attention of Western people, of the majority of whom it would be true to say that their minds run in religious grooves, and they seem to be satisfied with conditioned thinking within a limited enclosure. Should we not be as keen to know what the great sages, saints and illuminated ones of Asia have taught about the great issues of life, as well as appreciating the teachings of those who have drawn their inspiration exclusively from the Judaeo-Christian sources?

For my own part – and I speak very humbly, but as one who has tried to survey the whole field – I am quite satisfied that reincarnation and karma are great key-truths to be reckoned with. Their truth illumines human life, death and destiny, and without these keys it seems to me there can be no comprehensive and satisfactory philosophy of human life.

I am quite aware that the popular attitude to the issue of reincarnation is expressed by the question, 'Have I lived on earth before'? This is immediately followed by the further question 'If so, who was I, and when and where did this take place'? This popular attitude towards karma treats the subject as a sort of celestial bank account whose healthy or unhealthy state reflects the moral credits or debits we have incurred in our past-lives. An approach which is not unreasonable, but it is elementary and immature, for it is placing the emphasis on the succession of transient personalities rather than viewing them all as fragments of a long process in time that is concerned only with the unfolding and maturing of the soul.

Every great master who guides his pupils along the upward spiritual path will remind them from time to time that he is not on earth to pamper their personalities, but in the interests of their immortal souls which are precious to the Father, and which He wants to lead Home.

Let us for a moment try to take a cosmic view. The ancient Hindu sages have envisaged the Creator as alternatively manifesting a kind of 'breathing out' and then a 'breathing in' followed by a rest period before the cycle begins again. This huge period of perhaps billions of years is called by them a manvantara. In the phase which has been called a 'breathing out' universal creation and evolution of forms takes place, while the 'breathing in' phase had been called involution or reabsorption. The soul goes through a small-scale cycle in time corresponding to the cycle of the cosmos. The great descending process of the soul, from the high level of its first creation to the physical level, corresponds to evolution or the 'breathing out', while its reascent to the divine levels corresponds to the involution or 'breathing-in'. The souls of men fall like grains of wheat into the soil of earth to unfold their divine potentialities. This 'fall' of men involves the soul in increasing restriction in space, time and freedom. It involves increasing separation and aloneness, and especially through the aloneness of suffering souls learn things which they could not know otherwise. Through restriction in space and time they learn to know of the infinite and the eternal; through suffering they come to know of compassion and love.

26

The soul that distils wisdom from each personality manifestation becomes enriched, evolved and god-like, as it returns and offers itself to the One. The Irish mystic and poet AE must have had these thoughts in his mind when he wrote, 'Our spring and our summer are an unfolding into life and form, and our autumn and winter are a fading into the Infinite Soul.' He once questioned his soul 'To what end is this life poured forth and withdrawn?' and he received the answer: 'The End is creation, and creation is Joy. The One awakens out of quiescence as we come forth, and knows itself in us: as we return, we enter It in gladness, knowing ourselves.' . . . This is indeed a profound thought.

Students of psychic research are well aware that during the last fifty years much thoroughly scientific work has been done in the field of precognition. This is the term used of the faculty of foreseeing the future where there are no past regularities from which inferences can be drawn. We know that observations of past regularities allow scientists to predict high tides, eclipses, phases of the moon, the return of comets, etc. – but foreknowledge of other events such as the dates of cyclones, earthquakes, storms, deaths of persons, crashes of planes, accidents to trains or cars or ships cannot be based on any past regularities.

I quote two eminent investigators whose views merit respect. Dr Richet an eminent physiologist and Nobel prizeman, said of precognition, 'It is demonstrated verity. It is a strange, paradoxical and seemingly absurd fact, but one that we are compelled to admit'. Dr Eugene Osty after a lifetime's work with mediums affirmed 'There is a transcendental stratum or principle in all human beings which shows that it is aware of the individual life, and is capable of foreknowing its circumstantial development'. You may be thinking: 'Why have you changed the subject? I thought you were discussing karma, but suddenly you branch off into the theme of precognition.' I have done this because I want to suggest to you that reliable evidence for precognition strongly supports the idea of karma.

That which can be, and sometimes is, precognised can only be the karmic pattern of events precipitated from it. We have therefore in this field of psychical research independent evidence of the principle of karma. The foreseeable future is not however a rigidly fixed one that *must* be. It is malleable by new attitudes or choices of one's self and possibly by other beings who may be willing to operate within their specious present on a higher level of consciousness than ours.

If you are convinced, as I am, that reincarnation and karma are twin principles or truths which illumine our life, there is one supremely important question you will ask – and it must be answered – 'What is the meaning of life? What is the goal of life? How can it in fact be achieved?' I am devoting a future chapter to this question and calling it *The Soul's Great Journey* but I must introduce the question and its answer now.

Shakespeare once said, 'All the world's a stage, and all the men and women merely players. They have their exits and their entrances . . .' The 'exits' we call death, and the 'entrances' we call birth. It is said that most men fear death and most discarnate souls fear birth. But perhaps a true appreciation of the twin principles of reincarnation and karma would help to remove both these fears. For why should we, as souls, fear to do once more what we have done already so many times before?

What is this whole pageant about, which leads over half a million to born on the planet each day? One of the old Indian Scriptures, the Upanishads, was inspired to say of the act of original creation, 'Out of Joy all things proceed, by Joy they are preserved, and into Joy they enter at last and find their Goal.' Of course we can do no more than speculate here, but it would seem that out of the fullness of His joy and love, the Creator aeons of time ago sent forth myriads of germinal cells, or youthful souls, each capable of evolving into God-likeness. As a great oak tree gives rise to a myriad of acorns, each of which has the potentiality of growing into a giant oak provided it is detached from the parent tree and is subject to rain and storm and the nourishment of earth, so myriads of germinal souls were created by God and given their freedom from God. To be given 'their freedom from God' may seem a strange phrase unless we remember that the acorn has its freedom from the oak tree which gave it birth, but it embodies the same essential principle of 'oakness'. God is absolutely free, and His created souls were given their freedom. It is through this gift of the power to choose that they grow and evolve. It is only far later in the journey through time, at a much later stage of evolution, that they surrender this freedom by saying 'Thy will be done, not mine'.

After this creation of souls on the level of spirit the wave of creation moved 'outwards and downwards' – I use these spatial terms for lack of anything better – and a whole universe of a lesser degree of reality was created. This universe we call 'mind'. Still later in time the wave of creation rolled further 'outward and downward' to create a universe of still lesser reality and this we call 'matter'. For purposes of exposition we need to subdivide these regions further, but for the present, the diagram

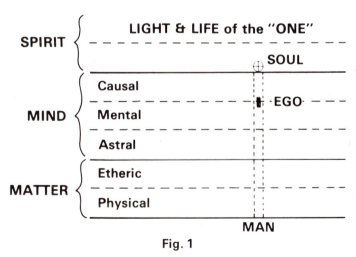

Fig. 1

shows us all we are discussing.

The diagram is indeed for me a key to the understanding of existence, and all I know about being and becoming finds a place in it. After their creation, these myriads of germinal souls were free to remain in their own country of spirit, or to explore for themselves the vast universe of mind. But once they crossed the threshold – as all those we call human did – several things resulted. (i) They appropriated for themselves a mental body to become an instrument of the soul's exploration in this universe. (ii) there was no stepping back or return: they had to go on (iii) they were now involved in the time-process, and (iv) they were in the world of opposites and came to know good and evil, light and dark, love and hate, strife and peace, etc., etc.

Of the great descent through aeons of time, we know but little and can only speculate. There are veiled symbolic references to some stages in early chapters of the Book of Genesis. I will mention briefly a few of these, but will not dwell upon them now. There is the eating of the magic fruit of the tree of knowledge of good and evil. The symbolism is telling us that the moral law is now placed *within*, and moral responsibility has to be accepted. Clearly karma is beginning. Note that Adam and Eve are then driven out of the garden of Innocence 'lest they should eat of the tree of eternal life' or immortality. In other words, there were to be no short cuts available back to the universe of spirit. The endowment of conscious immortality had now to be earned.

As our diagram indicates, souls in the age-long process of descent, each acquired a body or vehicle composed of the stuff of the realm which it was exploring. These vehicles or bodies, necessary as they were to gather knowledge and skill to operate in each realm, became in the end the prison walls of the soul. Having acquired an astral body, there remained the final step downward into matter – a step which resulted in the maximum restriction and limitation. To make this possible, powerful forces or shall we say powerful beings in the universe of mind had been experimenting for ages with material forms which they endowed with mind and thereby made them alive.

30

The whole story of their success is the familiar story of evolution recorded in biological text books. Starting with single-celled organisms like the amoeba, through endless experimenting and the process of trial and error – which biologists describe as the survival of the fittest – this fascinating biosphere with all its creatures, had been produced. The most intelligent and therefore most promising of these creatures was a mammal which might be called the anthropoid ape. Of living creatures it was not the largest, nor the toughest, nor even the most sensitive, but it had kept its future options open, it had a better brain, and could adapt itelf to environmental change. Its fine brain permitted mind to operate through it with considerable success. It was into this creature that the final stage of descent of the soul and its vehicles (down to the astral one) took place. Man, or homosapiens as he is called, was therefore the meeting of two streams of consciousness – the soul and its higher vehicles which had descended, and the anthropoid ape which had ascended.

The physical order is the lowest level of man's imprisonment. It is the far country referred to in the parable of the prodigal son. This parable is of course a cosmic myth which presents certain features of the process of the ascent of man, once he has become utterly disillusioned and tired by the far country – this material order. It is true that the light and life of the One penetrate downwards to the lowest level where incarnate souls are in exile, but the light of the lamp of the soul is wrapped round by so many veils – which we call bodies – that it is relatively dim and unnoticed to those who are on earth.

The great task of the return of the soul to its native country – the universe of spirit – which is what Jesus called the Kingdom of God, is what we are all here to undertake. We have fallen far from those realms of light which our souls once knew, and to return there, which is every soul's deepest longing, is a long and arduous journey. What this involves I shall talk about in later chapters, but the hardest work has to be done here on the physical level where the conditions are severest.

I think with this concept of man's origins we can see the place of reincarnation and karma. Does anyone honestly think that at the end of one life here he is fully evolved in his soul-consiousness, that he has learned all that life has to teach him and he is fit and ready to know God and enter into the glory and holiness of the Supreme One? The very idea is absurd. All incarnate souls therefore at death − which is simply a casting-off of the physical and etheric bodies − enjoy life for a time on one of the astral levels of which there are many. According to the soul's needs it may spend a few years or many centuries there, until at last the urge towards change comes strongly enough. The forces that make for rebirth are then set in operation and those advanced souls sometimes called the Lords of Karma direct the soul that is to be reborn to the right parents at the right time.

By 'right' I mean the situation which will offer to the soul the best opportunity of discharging some of its karmic debts and making progress towards the final goal. Thus the Wheel of Births and Deaths, as the Hindus call it, is ever turning and brings us once more into the company of those to whom we have been linked in the past by many and various emotional ties. Always the soul hopes afresh when it returns, that this time it will make real progress towards the great goal of life. Sometimes it does, but alas, how often the old ego quickly takes control and once more we waste our opportunities!

Very few people know what they are living for. If you were to interview a sample you would certainly obtain a variety of answers. Many would say, if they were honest, that they are living to get as much pleasure out of life as possible. By implication they are not looking beyond this present life, and if challenged, most would probably say that they are not sure whether there is anything beyond it. Certainly each of these is the centre of his own little world which the selfish ego rules. Many others may confess that they like power and success. Such power may take many different forms: the accumulation of money, the acquirement of skills, the accumulation of knowledge and fame, positions of leadership and over-rule. These persons are all on what is called the path of desire, i.e., they are all on the turning wheel of births and deaths. It is largely unfulfilled desire which draws men back again and again to Earth. All the great Eastern teachers are continually drawing their disciple's attention to this, as, for example Krishna does in the *Bhagavad Gita*. Then there is another large group in the sample who will say that they want to help or serve mankind. This is certainly a step higher – spiritually speaking – than the pursuit of happiness and power for the self. But how often this 'doing good' is linked with self! The doer likes his works to be noticed; he likes credit for it; he is not content to be unknown or let others have the praise. Then there is a very small group who are moving on the path of light, unconcerned with pleasure or power or success as the world counts it. They are content to say, with the Irish mystic AE, 'My friend, a man's success or failure is always with his own soul'.

Can we suppose that the activities of modern man, complex though they are, go deeply enough to satisfy him? Does he feel content to remain a cog in a huge machine called Society, and to repeat what myriads of others have done to keep the wheels of civilisation turning? Is it satisfying to what is deep within him to be born – without conscious choice – to have some education, to enjoy some pleasures and excitements, to have a family, to make a few friends, to find himself ageing, to hand responsibilities over, and to wait for the end of life? Billions have done this, and to what end? Have they been pursuing any meaningful goal above the flux of change, and rooted in the eternal? Is there not deep down in everyone a longing for meaning, a buried hunger for something unknown that has nothing to do with the world's tumult, conflict and suffering?

As with one voice, the great teachers of mankind have said, 'Of course there is. The meaning of life is found in being, not in doing. Each soul is a centre of being, still in seed form and

33

possibly unawakened, but waiting to unfold its God-like potentialities. On this physical level of the world the soul is entangled in restrictions although they can be surmounted given enough desire and will to do so. This level is the soil in which and out of which the seed of being has to germinate and grow before it can emerge into the Divine Light.' Our task as mortals is first to realise our real situation, and then to start the journey that will lead us back at last to those high levels of consciousness, the 'Father's Kingdom' that we once left.

You may recall that Gautama the Buddha regarded spiritual ignorance as the great tragedy of man. And, as you know, suffering is the great awakener of men. I think we are going to go through a period of great suffering, in the interest of our souls – which must be awakened to the meaning of life. I shall quote to you as I conclude, a saying of Pythagoras, 'Take courage, for the race of man is divine.'

The Certainty of Survival of Death

If it is true that man perishes with the death of his physical body, let us frankly admit that we live in a world which is deplorably and fundamentally unjust to many people, and which is tragically disturbing to every thoughtful person. Some people have had major handicaps through life; some have contended with frustration, suffering, poverty, cruelty and discouragement. Some have fought gallantly, and to what end – if character perishes with death? An observer of human life to whom moral justice is all-important, can offer us no comfort if his horizon is bounded by this life.

Even for the most fortunate of men, if we perish when the body dies, then the things we have most valued when alive, the love we have known and given, the beauty at whose shrine we have worshipped, the sacrifices which others have made for us – these things must bring to us our saddest thoughts. I take it therefore that there is no more urgent question we can ask than this: 'Do I survive death in the fullness of my powers?' I think we have a right to expect an answer satisfying alike to our thinking and feeling.

May I first point out that some persons are in a fortunate position. They can say to us with complete conviction, 'I *know* I shall survive death.' For example, those who are quite convinced of the truth of reincarnation, perhaps through former life-memories, will be in this position. For what their soul has done perhaps hundreds of times before, there is no ground for doubting it can do again and again. Survival is implicit in reincarnation.

Then there are quite a number of people who have had personal experiences of 'astral projection' or out-of-the-body experiences. They, their higher and true self, may have wandered out of the sleeping vehicle which is called the body, and in their astral body have felt full consciousness and freedom to explore the physical levels or the near astral levels. I have met scores of such persons and hundreds of records of this phenomenon have been made and studied. Dr Robert Crookall's books are well known, and I devoted Chapter 10 of my book *The Imprisoned Splendour* to the subject. To those persons there can be no reasonable doubt that consciousness does not depend upon the physical brain and body, but that they possess a vehicle in which they can function with far wider powers than those they have used in their physical one.

Then, here and there, one is privileged to meet a mystic. He may be nominally a Christian, a Hindu, a Buddhist, a Sufi, or may have no outer label. But he is a person who has lifted consciousness inwardly to higher levels than mind. These comparatively rare souls have immediate access to truth quite other than through the intellect. When they speak of lower levels they do so with an authority which one recognises intuitively. A true master, for example, would seldom, if ever, spend time talking about survival. To him it is self-evident. If he has been teaching about a loving God Who cares for all His children eternally, it would be irrelevant nonsense to discuss whether He still cared for them after they had discarded their physical bodies.

Apart from the groups of people to which I have referred there are very many others to whom I am particularly addressing myself in this book. I can imagine some of them saying, 'We are perhaps unfortunate. We have not enjoyed the experiences of which you have spoken. We have no certain memories of past lives. We are not mystics. We have not had out-of-the-body experience that we can remember. We do not even find faith coming easily. We don't want to be led up the garden-path, but we are open to weigh evidence and, if you can show us some good evidence, then even though we may not find it conclusive as proof, we may be able to live with it as a working hypothesis. But is there such evidence?'

In this chapter I am going to assert that there is plenty of very good evidence, and present you with examples of it. I get a bit tired of hearing eminent persons making pontifical statements in fields which they have never taken the trouble to study. One eminent philosopher who believes that death ends all has made no secret of his intention of 'building his house on the firm foundations of unyielding despair', and has said more recently, 'I can see no reason whatever to suppose that the universe takes any interest in our hopes and desires'. But I have found no evidence that he has ever studied the good evidence that would have given him solid ground for a different outlook.

If you started to receive communications allegedly from a friend who had gone to live in another country, could you satisfy yourself that they were from your friend? I think most people would say 'Yes'. I suggest that you would be able to form a sound opinion based upon such things as (i) memories you shared in common, but had not shared with anyone else who might conceivably impersonate your friend. (ii) personal characteristics such as moral outlook, sensitivity, views and ideals and interests in common, type of reaction to things, sense of humour, peculiarities of phrasing, speech, and outlook, etc. Each of our known friends is a different personality which we recognise as such. Now in the case where we have lost by death a good friend, the problem is not one of distance but that his consciousness and mine are now normally focussed on two different levels.

This brings us to consider the nature of mediumship which is a phenomenon which makes it possible to bridge this gulf. There are persons – not very uncommon – who can withdraw consciousness slightly or substantially from the physical brain-level to a level of the mind called generally the astral level. This is the normal level to which we pass after physical death. Such a type of withdrawal is called trance, and persons who find this easy to do are usually called mediums or sometimes 'sensitives'. If we sit with such a medium, he or she may become a go-between and may be used by our deceased friend to communicate with us. There appear to be two different methods used, or often something which is a combination of them both. One is the establishment of a telepathic link between the *mind* of our friend and the *mind* of the medium.

The communication is thus on the thought-level and it is left to the medium to find words to express by speaking or writing, what the communicator conveys. The second method is one in which the *mind* of the communicator influences the *brain* of the medium, her own mind having partially withdrawn to make this possible. In this latter type there may be speech or writing characteristics peculiarly associated with the deceased communicator. There is an interesting case where Oscar Wilde purported to communicate through a medium (who was not familiar with Wilde's handwriting). The so-called automatic scripts were compared later with an autograph letter written by Wilde when alive, and there was no mistaking the identity. Many forms of communication blend in different degrees the mind-to-mind and the mind-to-brain relationship.

It might be of interest if I mention my own personal experiences with a well-known medium in London, Miss Geraldine Cummins. My wife and I met her for the first, and only, time in October 1953. It was a social occasion, and before leaving I asked Miss Cummins, my hostess, if sometime she would try to get some writing from the other side that would be of interest to me. She graciously agreed to do so, but asked me if I would give her a sample of my handwriting to be a psychic link with me. This I did. About five months later in Melbourne in March 1954, I received a letter from Miss Cummins saying that holding my sample of handwriting in one hand and withdrawing into a quiet state she had written with the other the enclosed script.

This purported to be from Astor, a control of the medium, who gave me a description in a few words, of a friend of mine, Ambrose Pratt, who had died in Melbourne about 10 years before this. Astor gave me his name from symbols which were shown to him. All Astor's statements were correct. I was very impressed, wrote to thank Miss Cummins and asked her if she would try again to contact him. Before she did so I asked her to read a letter which I enclosed and in which I wrote to my friend Ambrose Pratt just as though he were alive and able to read it. I suggested that if she – Miss Cummins – would read it, then Ambrose Pratt would be able to know its contents from her mind, and could answer the questions I asked him through her automatic writing.

Some weeks later I received another automatic script from Miss Cummins. In this, the questions I asked were reasonably answered. The most remarkable feature of this script was, however, that after writing two or three lines Astor said he would relinquish the pen to Ambrose and let him write. The handwriting changed markedly and suddenly to something not very unlike the medium's normal handwriting – and from this I concluded that the link-up was chiefly telepathic, that Ambrose was dropping thoughts into the medium's mind. This is not the time or place to go into more detail, but I have told the story in my book *The Light and the Gate*. I will only say this. He told me that he had come from farther regions of spirit-life because he had certain directions to give me. He had certain links with a group of scholars on his side of death – he named half a dozen of them – and said he was in touch with me on their behalf. They asked me to study the philosophical work of Douglas Fawcett – a little-known philosopher, still alive in Chelsea aged about 90, and to write an exposition of it for the thoughtful man of today.

This task I undertook and it resulted in the book *Nurslings of Immortality*. During the following four or five years I received many communications from my friend. He was an able and distinguished man and the style and authority with which he wrote reminded me forcibly of the man I had known when alive. I need only say without more ado that I became convinced that I had been in touch with my old friend Ambrose Pratt.

To the sceptic who may suggest that the correct description of my friend and his interests might have been a brilliant piece of thought-reading of my mind by Miss Cummins – she being in England and I being in Australia – I can only say that this hypothesis does not impress favourably bacause of some subtle features that the scripts present. Furthermore, I knew nothing at the time about Douglas Fawcett or his philosophic ideas, and nothing could have been farther from my mind than the suggestion that I should want to expound his thought! I was quite convinced by these scripts of the survival of my friend.

Now let us look a little further at mediumship in general. The fundamental question raised by all good mediumship is this. When an enquirer sits with a medium and hopes to contact a deceased friend it may happen that the medium does present a lot of material, descriptive of the deceased friend, and also many memories shared between the sitter and this deceased friend. The sitter may be duly impressed. But does this mean that the deceased friend has communicated this information through the medium, or does it mean that the medium in trance has telepathically drawn the information from the sitter's unconscious mind and presented it back to the sitter? Both would appear possibilities and therefore such mediumship does not offer any certain proof of survival of the deceased friend and communication with him or her.

To make it less likely that the information was withdrawn telepathically by the medium from the sitter's mind, experiments were made with proxy sitters. The idea was, that someone should go and sit with the medium on behalf of the enquirer, and that this person sitting should know perhaps only the name of the deceased friend, and nothing more. If a lot of information was communicated it would then appear more likely that it was the deceased friend who was the source of it. But a sceptic could quite justifiably say that the medium might have read from the sitter's mind on whose behalf the proxy had come, and then draw the information from this proxy's mind.

Someone may say, 'Why couldn't a deceased communicator disclose something which *he* knew, but which no living person knows; but something that could be later verified by the research of the sitter'? For example, a person before his death took a brick, made certain marks upon it for identification, broke it in two and gave one half-brick to his sister. He told his sister he proposed to bury the other half-brick and disclose where he had hidden it after his death, if this were possible. It was done successfully. But was this absolute proof of the survival of the one person who had this knowledge? It might be claimed that the medium in trance had exercised clairvoyant faculty and discovered its whereabouts.

There is another type of experiment called 'book tests', but they are capable of being criticised along the same lines as that just given. I present however a case which strongly suggests survival. Lady Pamela Glenconner sat with the well-known medium Mrs Osborne Leonard. One of Lady Glenconner's sons Edward Wyndham Tennant, known within the family by the nickname 'Bim', had been killed in the Battle of the Somme in 1916. His father Lord Glenconner was extremely interested in forestry and planned and tended the forest areas on his estates with care. Lady Glenconner records how, often when walking in the forests, her husband would depressingly remark that all the young shoots were being ruined by the beetles: it was the greatest pest they had to contend with etc. So familiar was this theme to the family that if his father was pessimistic about anything, Bim would say 'All the woods have got the beetle'. It was a homely instance of a family joke, peculiarly characteristic of Bim.

Now at this particular sitting with Mrs Leonard, her control Feda said after giving other messages, 'Bim now wants to send a message to his father. Underline that, he says. It is in the 9th book on the 3rd shelf counting from left to right in the bookcase on the right of the door in the drawing room as you enter. Take the title and look at p. 37.'

The book indicated was in fact *Trees* (by J. H. Kelman)

41

and on p. 36 at the bottom leading on to p. 37 were the words, 'Sometimes you will see curious marks in the wood; these are caused by a tunnelling beetle very injurious to the trees.' Lady Glenconner remarks, 'Had a chance observer been present when we traced this test, he would have said, "This is no mourning family, these are happy people" and he would have been right.'

This case is certainly an impressive one, and I would myself accept as very highly probable that it was evidence of Bim's survival. But it is not absolute proof, for the medium's mind might have searched round telepathically in Lady Glenconner's mind, found this homely illustration and then exercised a most remarkable power of clairvoyance to find a book test to support it.

A remarkable experiment was carried out early in the century by Dr Richard Hodgson, a very competent investigator with a sceptical turn of mind. He had a friend George Pelham. After Pelham died he communicated with Dr Hodgson for several years through the mediumship of Mrs Piper, a famous American medium. Dr Hodgson drew up a lengthy report of this work and declared, in the end, that he was convinced beyond any doubt of the survival of his friend George Pelham. Dr Hodgson's approach was essentially scientific and one among the many tests he made over the years of study was to take with him at one time or another no less than 150 persons to sittings with Mrs Piper.

Thirty of these had been personal friends of Pelham when alive on earth. He recognised each of them, and conversed with each on matters of mutual interest, showing the appropriate knowledge and degree of intimacy. Of the other 120 persons he made no false recognition or mistakes. This sort of evidence is very impressive in a psychological sense, as we all recognise that with our various friends we share differing mutual interests and different degrees of friendship.

There is another type of communication which occasionally happens through a medium, and it can be an extremely impressive pointer to the survival of a personality with its wishes, loves, concerns, memories etc. Sometimes a medium will give a sitting, and communication is taking place, when suddenly this is interrupted by another communicator breaking in. He is generally not known or recognised by the medium or sitters, but he is desperately anxious to get in touch with someone on earth, and asks for cooperation. Such motives are frequently to warn someone of a great danger, to make amends for a wrong done, to help someone in great distress through a crisis, etc. I shall relate one of the best cases I know. I owe it to a correspondent Mr Norman Hunt and he has given me permission to use it. He told me that for many years he had carefully studied mediumship in his own home in Kent, England using tape-recorders etc., and that he met weekly with some friends in a little home circle. One member of his circle was a lady from Czechoslovakia whom he calls Edith in the account he gave me.

On this occasion Edith was quite unexpectedly controlled in a trance by a person who gave his name as C—. He appeared very anxious indeed that we should try to help his wife, who he said, had been arrested and was then in prison in Prague, the name of which he gave us. If someone would get into touch with a certain Dr K— whose name and address he gave us – he said that Dr K had access to documents which could secure his wife's release from prison.

On returning to ordinary consciousness Edith was told of this. She had only slight knowledge of the communicator C, but had heard that he had died. Edith was unaware of the other circumstances, of the fate of C's wife, or even of the existence of a Dr K. Feeling a moral obligation to do something to help, Edith wrote a guarded letter because of the political implications. She received back from Dr K, a rather angry letter telling her not to meddle in dangerous business. There the matter rested for about 18 months, when a former acquintance of Edith who had also known the late C—, escaped from Czechoslovakia and made his way to England. He sought Edith out, and told her the following story.

He said the late C— had three daughters. At his death, the youngest had only been 11 months old. When this little girl was only 3 or 4 she was found to be writing little messages which she said came from her daddy. She insisted that he was constantly present in the house. She started to hold conversations with him and said she could see him plainly and describe him. Her family rejected the whole thing as fantastic, and the child's supposed mental state became a source of anxiety to them. The narrator (the person talking to Edith) went on to say that he had visited the family of C— in Prague. He explained to them that he was a member of a spiritualistic circle in Prague, that a person called C— had spoken through their medium and had asked that some member of the circle should pay a visit to his family. He was now doing this in fulfilment of C's request. C— had made two requests. The first was that his youngest daughter should be allowed to visit their circle. This was granted, and the youngest daughter of C was shown a photograph of a group of people and asked if she knew any of them. She correctly picked C— from this photograph and said, 'That's my papa who comes and talks to me'. C's second request was that someone in their circle should contact a certain Dr K giving his name and address, as he had access to certain papers which could secure his wife's release from prison. Apparently Dr K was in a better mood and he sent on these papers to the Public Prosecutor in whose hands the case of C's wife rested. Shortly afterwards she was released from prison.

This kind of evidence where seperate events took place, all converging on an event in which the communicator had every reason to be profoundly interested, points very strongly indeed to the survival of C.

This sense of urgency and compelling motive may show itself in ways other than intrusion into a seance. I will relate an account vouched for by my friend Dr Leslie Weatherhead.

The incident happened to a colleague of his.

A minister was sitting alone in his study one night when he heard the bell ring. Going to the door he found standing there a young woman whom he knew fairly well. She was from a village some five miles away. The village was in an adjoining circuit from which the minister had moved some sixteen months before.

'Good evening' she cried, 'I expect you have forgotten me but I have come on a very urgent errand. My father is dying. He never attended church much, but once or twice when you were in the circuit we persuaded him to hear you preach. I do wish you would come and pray with him before he passes away.

'I will come at once' replied the minister. Putting on his hat and coat and taking an umbrella from the stand, he set off in the pouring rain on a five mile walk accompanied by the young woman.

On his arrival at the house, the wife welcomed him warmly. 'Oh, how good of you to come' she said, 'but how did you know that my husband was passing away?'

'Your daughter came for me' he replied, with some surprise at the question. It was the woman's turn to be surprised now.

'Come upstairs at once' she said, 'and we will talk afterwards'.

The minister went to the bedside of the dying man, spoke to him and prayed with him, and shortly afterwards, the end came. Turning to the woman who was now a widow, he asked where the daughter was, for he had not seen her again since they entered the house. The woman replied, 'I was surprised when you came to the door this evening, and I asked you who told you that my husband was dying. You said that my daughter called, and that you had come out together. You have not heard then that my daughter died a year ago?'

Now the minister was astonished indeed. 'Dead!' he exclaimed, 'she came to my door, rang the bell, and walked out here with me.'

45

'But there,' he said, 'I think I can prove that. As we came along together, the road was up at one place, and a watchman and another man were sitting in a hut in front of a fire. They saw us go by. I'll speak to them on my way home.'

He set off on his return journey, and found the two men still sitting in front of the fire. 'You saw me go by an hour or so ago didn't you?' he said to the men. 'Was I alone?' 'Yes sir', one of them replied, 'and you were talking away to yourself as fast as you could go.'

If you do not accept the basic idea of the survival of the dead daughter you will have difficulty in accounting for the data presented.

Sometimes the intervention of the discarnate may arise in dream experience as in the case of the famous Chaffin will. But we shall not pursue this type of evidence further. There is however a field of research which was actively conducted in the years 1907–1916 by the Society for Psychical Research in London. It is known as the Cross-Correspondence experiment. Its vital importance can only be assessed properly by those who are willing to study the records in detail. The material for doing this is all preserved in the Proceedings of the Society.

I shall attempt to give a simple appreciation of this work, since it does in my view, offer very strong evidence of survival of death in the fullness of one's powers. Among the group of half a dozen scholars and friends at Cambridge who founded the Society I have just referred to, was a well-known classical scholar and minor poet and author F. W. H. Myers. He died in 1901, and when incarnate had been as active as anyone in assessing and collecting data bearing on the subject of proving survival. Associated with the Society about this time were several ladies who had some mediumistic capacity which took the form of 'automatic' or, if you like, 'inspired' writing. The facts that I will present to you suggest that the deceased Myers was the author of this experiment from the other side.

He composed an erudite classical essay and communicated one part of it through the automatism of one of the ladies, another part of it through a second, and the remainder through a third lady. He introduced a number of allusions and cross-references in each of these parts, but of course the three recipients could make very little sense of what was communicated. Each of them• sent their queer communications to the Headquarters of the Society and there it was seen that they were inter-linked. Classical scholars who examined them were able to show that the parts fitted together to make an intelligent whole.

Perhaps an analogy will help. If one had a large jig-saw puzzle, shuffled it and divided the pieces into three piles, asking three seperate people to make what they could of their pile – it is clear that each effort would be very fragmentary and incomplete until the three efforts were brought together and examined. If it then appeared that they make one complete whole, the inference would be that a single intelligent person was responsible for all of the fragments. This type of experiment with classical essays was made several times and those best qualified to judge formed the opinion that Myers was indeed the author and was attempting from the other side of death to present the strongest possible evidence of his survival. I personally think he achieved this.

The case for survival does not rest upon a few examples such as we have looked at, and hundreds of others like them, but upon many lines of converging evidence. It is rather paradoxical that our present knowledge of the extra-sensory powers of mind-telepathy, clairvoyance, precognition etc. – makes it very difficult to devise an absolutely conclusive test of survival, while at the same time the very existence of these powers of the mind make it less and less likely that the mind has any essential dependence upon matter. Absolute scientific proof may be impossible: perhaps all that intellect and mind can offer is evidence pointing to a very high probability of survival. For practical purposes this is all we need, and with this awareness we can start to make sense of the world we know.

In the light of a destiny which we conceive as extending far beyond death and birth we need not entertain fears that the world is meaningless or fundamentally unjust to the individual. We can see our present experience as part of a far greater whole which stretches beyond both the portals of birth and death.

Every soul, once it has got past the stage of transition, has the opportunity given to it to assess it past life and the lives which have gone before. Metaphorically it might be described as an intimate film of the life, starting with the last phase and moving back to the earliest stages. But it is an experience in which we have to enter into the effects of our actions on others and the feelings engendered by them. In this way we see what we have done and become aware of the pattern and our deviations from it. It is no external judgement that we face but that of our own soul. As the poet expressed it:

> . . . he ever bears about
> A silent court of justice in himself:
> Himself the judge and jury, and
> Himself the prisoner at the bar.

Up to this point I have been concerned to present to you types of evidence which allow a sound judgement to be formed about our survival of death. In the remainder of this chapter I want to look at death from the human standpoint for it is an experience which we all must face not only for ourselves but for those we love. Since the lower self or ego has been fed throughout its life with sense-data, it feels sadness and grief at the disappearance of those we love. It looks like extinction – although it is not. The poet Tennyson expressed this poignant cry in a simple poem:

> Break, break, break,
> On the cold grey stones, O Sea!
> And I would that my tongue could utter
> The thoughts that arise in me,
>
> O well for the fisherman's boy,
> That he shouts with his sister at play!
> O well for the sailor lad,
> That he sings in his boat on the bay!

And the stately ships go on
  To their heaven under the hill:
But O for the touch of a vanish'd hand
  And the sound of a voice that is still.

Break, break, break,
  At the foot of thy crags O Sea!
But the tender grace of day that is dead
  Will never come back to me.

The poet feels that Nature will continue its ceaseless rhythms as the centuries come and go, but the love and fellowship which gave meaning to the poet's life have gone for ever. He is wrong of course, but he is expressing poignantly the age-old suffering of man facing the departure, for a time, of someone he loves. I suppose that until a man reaches enlightenment and is able to experience simultaneously the greater reality of higher levels and planes of consciousness and lesser degree of reality of the physical world, these emotions will remain poignant and strong. In a famous elegy written to commemorate the life and death of his friend Keats, Shelley was able at last to write:

Peace, peace! he is not dead, he doth not sleep –
He hath awakened from the dream of life –
'Tis we, who lost in stormy visions, keep
With phantoms an unprofitable strife.

To those whose souls are awakening from the dream of life, there can only be one purpose in coming again and again into a physical body, namely – to win our freedom from this cycle of necessity, this wheel of births and deaths. To win this we have to reach illumination here in a physical body: we have to rise above our ordinary brain-consciousness to the consciousness called by the Indians 'samadhi' or by Jesus Christ, the 'Kingdom of God'. If before the end of an earthly life a man or woman has not made some real progress towards this goal, then such a reincarnation may be considered a barren one, no matter what success the world ascribes to him. But if he or she has tried, he will meet the

49

transition of death like Bunyan's character Mr Valiant-for-Truth, with confidence and serenity. Bunyan makes his hero say, in what is probably one of the finest passages in English literature:

> Then said he, I am going to my Father's; and though with great difficulty I have got hither, yet now do I not repent me of all the troubles I have been at to arrive where I am. My sword I give to him that shall succeed me in my pilgrimage, and my courage and skill to him that can get it. My marks and scars I carry with me, to be a witness for me that I have fought His battles, Who will now be my rewarder.

> When the day that he must go hence was come, many accompanied him to the riverside, into which he went, he said, 'Death, where is thy sting?' And as he went down deeper he said, 'Grave, where is thy victory?' So he passed over, and all the trumpets sounded for him on the other side.

From a philosophic point of view the existence of the more real can never depend in any essential sense upon the less real. Thus soul does not depend causally upon mind, nor mind causally upon body. As I said at the beginning of this chapter, all knowledge is uncertain, except mystical knowledge, which is of the soul. Mystics who, in a high state of consciousness have experienced the eternal reality and Its essentially loving nature, can never afterwards live as though ignorant of this. This fact assures us of our own eternal nature: *we are precious to Him.* Indeed the idea that physical death, that is the discarding of the outer vehicle, could ever be the end to what constitutes the true nature of a loving human being is a fantastic notion. To be loved by Him is the guarantee of our immortality. I shall close now by quoting to you the views of some well-known figures upon our subject.

Goethe, the great German poet-philosopher-scientist, once said

The thought of death leaves me in perfect peace, for I have a firm conviction that our spirit is a being of indestructible nature: it works on from eternity to eternity; it is like the sun, which, though it seems to set to our mortal eyes, does not really set, but shines on perpetually.

Rabindranath Tagore the Indian poet-philosopher in one of his letters to his friend C. F. Andrews said,

The creative impulse of our soul must have new forms for its realisation. Death can continue to dwell in the same sepulchre, but life must increasingly outgrow its dwelling-place; otherwise the form gets the upper hand and becomes a prison. Man is immortal, therefore he must die endlessly. For life is a creative idea: it can only find itself in changing forms.

Perhaps the same idea was in the mind of Oliver Wendell Holmes when he wrote his poem called *The Chambered Nautilus.* I will quote only on the third and last verses:

Year after year beheld the silent toil
That spread his lustrous coil;
Still, as the spiral grew,
He left the past year's dwelling for the new,
Stole with soft step its shining archway through,
Built up its idle door,
Stretched in his last-found home, and
knew the old no more.

Build thee more stately mansions, O my Soul,
As the swift seasons roll!
Leave thy low-vaulted past!
Let each new temple nobler than the last,
Shut thee from heaven with a dome more vast,
Till thou at length art free;
Leaving thine outgrown shell by life's unresting sea.

If I may return to Tagore and quote him again here is a sentence expressing the same idea – that death is expansion, not extinction:

> Our life, like a river, strikes its banks not to find itself closed in by them, but to realise anew every moment that it has its unending opening towards the sea.

I shall conclude by quoting four verses from a poem written by a very courageous woman. The moving and tragic story of the Brontës – three girls and their brother who lived in semi-isolation in a lonely parsonage on the Yorkshire moors in the early 19th century – is well-known. Emily Brontë was, perhaps more than the others, a mystic. She died at the age of 39 and in her short and lonely life wrote some verse that was found, after her death, among her papers.

> No coward soul is mine,
> No trembler in the world's storm-troubled sphere;
> I see Heaven's glories shine,
> And faith shines equal, arming me from fear.
>
> O God within my breast,
> Almighty, ever present Deity!
> Life – that in me has rest
> As I – undying Life – have power in Thee!

> *************

> Though earth and man were gone,
> And suns and universes ceased to be,
> And Thou wert left alone,
> Every existence would exist in Thee.
>
> There is no room for death,
> Nor atom that his might could render void:
> Thou – Thou art being and Breath,
> And What Thou art may never be destroyed.

The Soul's Great Journey

It has been truly said that the Universe exists for the benefit of souls. In His aspect of Creator, the Almighty may be regarded as the author of a great drama. By His imagining, He created all creatures on all levels of being, and all the realms. At first the drama must have existed for Him alone, just as a human drama exists at first only in the artist's imagination. Then He gave it existence apart from Himself, i.e., a life of its own. His power sustained and preserved it. This is the stage of simple-consciousness. Later on, He conferred on some of the creatures self-consciousness, so that they knew they were conscious. These started to seek for meanings, and the Illuminated Ones who have come to earth from time to time have always taught mankind that the goal is cosmic consciousness.

This is immediate consciousness of our Creator, sometimes called enlightenment. The ancient Indian philosophers always taught THAT ART THOU. In a previous chapter we presented the levels or realms of varying degrees of reality in simple diagram. The level of spirit is alone absolutely real; the levels below this were created – each one being precipitated from the one above. The myriad souls created by God, were like germinal cells or seeds capable of unfolding into God-likeness, and they were given their freedom.

A great oak-tree sheds millions of acorns, but before they can manifest their principle of oakness they have to detach from the parent tree, fall into the earth, and be subject to the experience of these lower levels. So myriads of souls were given their freedom. The unfolding or evolution of their latent qualities involved their descent through many levels of lesser reality in the course of aeons of time. In each world level through which it passed, a soul acquired a body or vehicle of expression on that level. When finally it had descended to the physical level it would acquire an outer body of matter. The vehicles acquired restricted the soul more and more, so that on the lowest level, the soul is virtually the prisoner of its bodies, and to use Wordsworth's lines of the planet Earth:

> The homely nurse doth all she can
> To make her foster-child, her inmate, Man,
> Forget the glories he hath known
> And that imperial palace whence he came.

Not all souls took the human course of descent or arrived at the physical level. There is, for example, the Deva line of descent which is intimately concerned with the life of Nature, and sustains on the etheric level, spirits of earth, water, air and fire.

Let us look briefly at the human soul, a traveller setting out on the great journey. Once souls left the level of spirit where they were created by God, and crossed the threshold leading downward into the world of mind, they took an irrevocable step. They were free – so they were volunteers. It was their choice.

Each soul appropriated from the universal mind several vehicles. The causal body is the highest form of mind, sensitive and interfused with spirit. It is creative and intuitive, the storehouse of wisdom gathered on the journey, and the preserver of karma. A lower vehicle includes intellect, memory, and the instruments of power. The astral vehicle is the source of emotion and desire and has marked effects upon the physical levels. The etheric or vital body is the blueprint to which the physical must conform. It is easily seen by clairvoyants, possesses several circulations of energy chiefly connected with the health of the physical body.

When the threshold was crossed souls were caught in the time-process.

Souls found themselves more and more on levels in which

the great opposites were contending – good and evil; light and darkness; kindness and cruelty; strength and weakness; pride and humility; etc., etc. – the list is endless. 'Strife,' said Heraclitus, 'is the father of all things', and certainly this is true of the descending arc of the journey. Of this descending phase we know very little but references to it are clearly found in the myths and legends of the race. There are marked references in the Book of Genesis, for example. The eating of the magic fruit in the Garden of Eden which offered them knowledge of good and evil marked a stage in which the moral responsibility was transferred from obedience to a deity outside to obedience to the soul within. The concern of Adam and Eve when they were told that they were naked probably symbolises the nakedness of the soul, viz., that their souls had not yet acquired any restricting bodies, etc.

As the soul descended into the region of mind, a centre with which we commonly identify ourselves – called the ego – started to build-up. It is this ego-centre which makes its choice between the opposites, preferring one of them and rejecting the other. The ego says 'I want', 'I like', 'I think', 'I feel', etc. and rules the personality. It becomes in fact the focus of what we call selfishness, for it seeks its own interests and preservation. It is shrewd and cunning and powerful, and broadly speaking is opposed to the soul's ideals. With each reincarnation of the soul there is also the re-entry of this ego-self which has been built up to a great strength through past ages.

Each new-born child therefore needs considerable discipline in its early years – up to seven, and in some cases, ten years – done with firmness and with love. The idealism and qualities of the soul cannot show themselves and moderate the ego's influence until the physical brain is sufficiently developed at about puberty. The ego so to speak comes through in advance of the soul – with some years start – and adult man in general lives with his soul a prisoner of the vehicles. The ego is the gaoler: it seeks its own ends and is seldom willing to listen to the voice of the soul – which it disregards.

The ego takes the individual along the path of desire, and the pursuit of this in one of its many forms, may be the chief interest for hundreds of lives. The aim is at first to get as much pleasure out of life as possible; later on this may be followed by the pursuit of power in one form or another, the acquisition of power over others, rulership, money, influence, fame and skills. It is indeed the lure of unfulfilled desire which is a most powerful factor in drawing back souls into incarnation again. In so doing some karma of the past is met again, and some new karma likely to be created.

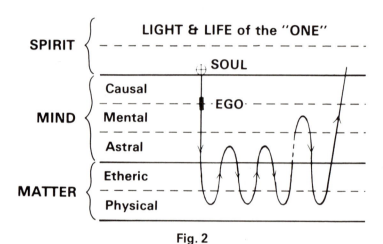

Fig. 2

Realising this, all true teachers lay much stress on the control of desire while on earth, exhorting their disciples to control their senses and root out desire. They know that if this hard task is not substantially achieved in this life, it is unlikely to be achieved on the astral levels where the pull of desires and emotions is much stronger — so that reincarnation is almost inevitable. The soul is bound to the ever-turning wheel of births and deaths. For life after life incarnate souls gathering experience, come at long last to see that power itself will never satisfy something deep within them. Souls then

56

often turn to more lives in which forms of service, and help to needy mankind, are important.

Often however this 'doing of good' is linked with satisfaction of the ego-self: the doer is still not content to offer his service to God, but likes it to be noticed so that he may receive credit for it in the eyes of men. But at last there does come a life or group of lives of disillusionment with the world. The ego is no longer attracted by or satisfied with anything the world offers. The world's attractions have all been found empty and tawdry, and in this mood the individual cries out in disillusion or depression, 'Vanity of vanities, all is vanity'. Some individuals start to seek intensely for the meaning of life. They search assiduously with mind and intellect until they realise at last that these are largely tools of the ego, and cannot by their nature lead them to the place of true peace and satisfaction. Some then withdraw into religious practices in ashram or monastery; some go in search of a guru or wise teacher whom they hope will point out the way and offer help and inspiration to the disciple.

Many are brought to this turning-point by suffering. Perhaps they are bereft of someone they deeply love, perhaps their plans are frustrated and their possessions destroyed. They come to the end of their tether and are brought painfully to realise, what the soul has always whispered to them, that there is no security or satisfaction in anything finite. How many lives of suffering, disillusionment, bitterness and darkness men inflict upon themselves before they make the discovery that their only security is God. Francis Thompson portrays this crisis perfectly in his great poem *The Hound of Heaven*, where the fugitive soul cries out:

Naked I wait Thy love's uplifted stroke!
My harness piece by piece Thou hast hewn from me
And smitten me to my knee;
I am defenceless utterly.

It is at this point of darkness and despair that Thompson makes the first dawn of light appear, and the first awareness that there is meaning and significance in his situation comes to him. He knows that his life-purpose is now somehow linked with 'the hid battlements of Eternity'. He has a glimpse of these, and sees, not a blind impersonal fate or chance, sweeping away all men's tenderest hopes and loftiest dreams, but some loving One, whose voice the winds and waves must obey . . . He learns enough through this glimpse to have grounds for trust. He is not yet clear of the darkness but he is moving in the right direction. You will recall how the fleeing soul makes a significant confession. She says,

> For though I knew His love, Who followed,
> Yet was I sore afraid
> Lest having Him, I might have nought beside.

Here is the great paradox of life. The spiritual path is one in which the divine love of man's souls is contending with the ego, the selfish ruler of the personality. What the ego imagines is going to be a great renunciation – having nought beside – leads to the supreme gift, the 'pearl of great price'. All that we egos have conceived as worth having shows itself up as illusion. The closing lines of Thompson's poem present the fugitive with sublime reassurance as the pursuing Voice says to him:

> All that I took from thee I did but take,
> Not for thy harms,
> But just that thou might'st seek it in My arms.
> All which thy child's mistake
> Fancies as lost, I have stored for thee at home:
> Rise, clasp My hand and come.

The same wisdom is found in the parable of Jesus called the Parable of the Prodigal Son. It is of course a cosmic myth referring to the soul of man and its great journey. The soul asks for its spiritual inheritance, and leaves its father's home for the far country which is the earth. This is the beginning of the great descent of which we spoke earlier. We are told nothing of this part of the journey, but it is related that after a long sojourn there, a famine arises and the soul finds itself degraded and in want. After enough suffering, some memory returns of its former state in its father's home, and this glimpse causes him in desperation to turn his steps homeward.

The parable emphasises the father's attitude to the returning soul. His love for the wanderer has been unchanged through this vast span of time. He sees him coming from afar, runs to meet him and gives him the warmest of welcomes. There is no criticism, no judgement, no 'Where have you been?' He is received back as a son with the words, 'This, my son, was dead and is alive again; he was lost and is found.'

It is surprising how frequently mythology presents some aspect of the soul's journey. Sometimes the soul is portrayed as a royal prince changed by some spell cast upon him into an ugly creature or an animal form. From this restriction he can only be freed by someone who loves him for his own sake.

In the *Bible of the World* edited by Baloo & Spiegelberg, you will find a poem called *The Hymn of the Soul*. It relates how a child, symbolising the soul, is given a bundle of jewels, but deprived of his bright robe and purple toga. He is sent forth into the material world by his parents who make a compact with him.

> If thou goest down into Egypt,
> And bringest the one pearl,
> Which is in the midst of the sea
> Hard by the loud-breathing serpent,
> Then shalt thou put on thy bright robe
> And thy toga, which is laid over it,
> And with thy brother, our next in rank,
> Thou shalt be heir in our kingdom

The hymn describes how he puts on the Egyptian garb, eats their food, serves their king, and forgets all about the pearl. His parents, perceiving this, formulate a plan to help him. A letter is sent, in the form of a bird, urging him to rise up from sleep, and reminding him of his home and his rank – 'thou art a son of kings', and recalling to his mind the pearl for which he had been sent to Egypt. His soul awakens and he remembers his mission. He captures the pearl and starts upon the return journey. Being guided by the light and love of the letter which shows him the way. He strips off the garments of Egypt.

At a certain point on the way towards home, he is met by his father's treasurers who have brought for him the bright robe and the toga – which till then, he had forgotten, since they were fashioned to fit him as a child in his father's house. As he faced it, suddenly the garment seemed to be his whole self. It is described in its jewelled beauty as having 'the image of the King of Kings depicted in full all over it'.

There is a great deal more in *The Hymn of the Soul*, but it is clearly a myth of the soul's descent and ascent. Jung's psychology lays much stress on the collective unconscious mind, the great storehouse of nature's know-how and the race's experience. Mythology is one avenue of expression of this archetypal wisdom, but even the dreams of modern man reflect it also. A friend of mine had a remarkable dream a few years ago, which I will relate to you.

I saw in my dream a magnificent carved door, and decided at length to see what was on the other side of it. I found myself to be in a huge cave full of fascinating objects which seemed to be somewhat like sculptures in the making. They were difficult to understand, as though they were at an early stage of creation. I heard the great door slowly close behind me. I then noticed a little card intimating that fuller information would be found on the floor below, so I went down the magnificent and spacious staircase to the floor below. I found there equally magnificent, but clearer and more developed forms of what had puzzled me upstairs. Then I went down another wonderful staircase on to a still lower floor, and found there more of these wonders – only still more shaped and evolved. Finally I reached the ground floor, and there was the fully developed work. After looking around with great interest, I thought the time had come for me to retrace my steps, but I could see no sign of the magnificent staircase anywhere. I looked everywhere and started to get concerned. I was rushing around, when suddenly, I saw my teacher sitting there in a chair, apparently quite unconcerned. I rushed up and said hastily, 'Do you know the way out?' but did not even wait to hear the answer, and rushed off again to seek further. This panic-stricken behaviour happened two or three times and then I put the question again and waited. The teacher said almost casually, 'I might.' He then got up slowly from his chair and said, 'Follow me.' He led me to a strange, ancient, inconspicuous staircase which I had not noticed before. It was very different from the one I had come down. We climbed on and on, and the dream seemed to end there.

My friend is keenly interested in the spiritual path, and his archetypal dream is telling us the same truth as many myths and allegories, and the parable of the Prodigal Son. The descent is easy and seductive: the way back is hard. The New Testament says, 'Strait *is* the gate and narrow *is* the way, which leadeth unto life, and few there be that find it.'

Well, here we are on earth in incarnation, as we have been many times before. We are all souls awakening to our destiny, or we should not be here today. Each time we have come, it has been the soul's great desire that this time we shall make some substantial progress towards the goal. The goal is getting home to the kingdom and the precondition of this is truly finding or knowing God while on this lowest physical level. You will remember Krishna's moving and compassionate cry over humanity: 'As the mighty wind, though moving everywhere, has no home but space, so have all these beings no home but Me.'

All awakening souls yearn for home in their moments of reflection: but at other times the illusions of this world hold them fast in their sleep. I quote again to you the words of AE the Irish mystic, who when pressed to leave Dublin for a wider sphere of activity in London, replied, 'My friend, a man's success or failure is always with his own soul.'

To use another simile, it is as though each soul is a divinely

61

conceived actor in a play written and stored within each germinal soul, and to be lived into being. At each reincarnation it is as though the Great Producer hands over the part to be played in this life, saying, 'Here it is. You have agreed to do it so do your best. Through this acting you will come at last to know your true self, and in so doing you will know Me, your Father. If you get lost in it, cry out to Me for help. I am close at hand and will always hear you.'

Human life is from a higher viewpoint a great act, but this work on the stage of human life makes it possible to know the reality which we are, and thus to know God. This is the fulfilment of innumerable lives, and is called illumination or the beatific vision. It gives the soul the passport to climb through all the levels of consciousness, casting off the bodies as it climbs and opening the gate to the eternal kingdom of God, to cosmic consciousness and absolute freedom.

As the pilgrim-mystic moves towards the mountain-top he may experience glimpses, insights and partial illuminations indicating that the veil is being a little drawn aside. He becomes very sensitive to God everywhere, partly revealed and partly hidden. The starry sky, running streams, majestic mountains, green grass, the colours of flowers, the sound of inspired music, and the great silence will proclaim their divine origin to such a pilgrim.

When a soul has had enough of the endlessly turning wheel of births and deaths; when it is sick of the ego-self, and yearns to return home, what must it do? I propose to devote the remainder of this chapter to four practical activities which will help us to move in the right direction.

First — have a good look from time to time at the ego-self. Second — learn to accept life remembering that it is a pre-formed karmic pattern. Third — cultivate the three golden virtues: love, trust, and humility and finally — cultivate serenity within the opposites through non-attachment.

Have a good look at the ego-self. This is the ruler of personality — the centre of selfhood built up through many lives. It is full of wants and desires, and as the name implies, of egotism. Satisfy yourself, by relentless searching, that you are here in this setting, facing the difficulties you have, because they are your karma. Don't blame others. It is true that most of our past is hidden from us in the deep unconscious, but at least let us be honest on the conscious level.

Are we proud, vain, selfish, angry, impatient, concerned first for our own comfort? Are we anxious, fearful, prone to judge others, critical, insensitive, self-righteous? There is a long list of possibilities, and to know ourselves truly is important. How can we fight things if we do not face their presence? It is quite a wrong reaction to become morbid, depressed or guilty at what we find. This is an old trick of the ego. Let us stop feeling guilty about anything in the past and live with God in the present. Father Fenelon once said wisely: 'It is mere self-love to be inconsolable at seeing one's imperfections.' Having faced our faults we then have the long-drawn out task of overcoming them, and probably the best method is to cultivate whenever possible the opposite virtue. If the fault is pride we must cultivate humanity. If it is fear or anxiety we must cultivate trust in God. If it is greed we must give away something we really value. If it is criticism of others we should consider whether we have projected on to others, faults which are present in ourselves, but repressed. If I feel I am better than others, perhaps I am self-righteous. Who am I to do this? Many spiritual teachers advocate spending five minutes at each day's close, looking back over events where we may have failed to react rightly. Every spiritual teacher stresses purification from the selfishness of the ego. This is the hardest of tasks, and there is no single point where one can relax and say the task is finished.

Learn to accept life, remembering that every individual has a pattern to follow, known to the soul before this life was entered upon. There is no such thing as chance or accident for human souls. All that presents itself to us is the outworking of our karma. A rebellious attitude to the life-situation, or resentfulness against it, is a false reaction born of ignorance. Only by acceptance of life can we tread the path

63

of wisdom, and there is no freewill on the physical level except to choose how we will react to that which karma ordains. To say or think: if only I had the gifts of *X* or the opportunities of *Y* is a form of delusive desire created by the ego. The Gita makes this clear when it says, 'It is better to do thine own duty, however lacking in merit, than to do that of another, even though efficiently. It is better to die doing one's own duty, for to do the duty of another is fraught with danger.'

We tend to be very short-sighted. We call situations 'good' or 'bad', meaning really that we like or dislike them. Yet we have to face the fact that while joy and happiness can teach us something, sorrow and suffering often teach us much more. If the ego is sufficiently battered to be willing to listen to the voice of the soul, who can say that what the world calls tragedy may not prove to be a blessing? We are obliged to recognise that this domain of the opposites is a school for character-building, and what we chose to call good and evil are both our teachers. To transcend them we have to learn to understand them. How could we learn fortitude if we were not subject to suffering? How could we learn courage if we did not know fear? How could we learn trust in God, if we have not discovered that all finite and earthly things can let us down?

Acceptance of life may be defined as an attitude of mind and heart based upon trust in God. The question is often asked, 'If I act so as to try to change the situation, does this mean that I am not accepting life? The answer is surely 'No'. I may certainly act outwardly, but it is the inner attitude which is important. Let me illustrate this. If I am ill does acceptance of my illness mean that I should not go to a good doctor? Surely not. It was my karma to suffer from the illness, but it was also part of my karma to know a good doctor who could diagnose my illness and treat it. Acceptance of life is an inner state which is unchanged whether I am cured or not. Take another example. If I pray for a situation to become different from what it is, am I accepting life?

It depends how I pray. If I pray to God on the assumption that I know what is best for me, this prayer may be dangerous: it is certainly presumptuous. But if I pray for grace to accept His will, and for guidance as to how and when I should act in the situation, then I am doing the best possible thing. The power that allowed this to happen may require me to learn some lesson through it, and when I have learned this, the outer situation may be changed. The key to acceptance is found in my attitude towards the results of my endeavour to change it. Most of our difficulties arise because we are not yet free from ego-desires. The rest arise because we have a sneaking suspicion that chance or accident occasionally intervene.

How foolish it is to assume that we can ever know what is best for a person. We do not know what is best for ourselves: how then can we presume to know what is best for anyone else? Recall that we have sometimes prayed for things which, in His mercy, God has denied to us. In contrast, recall that we have often passed through experiences which we would have preferred to avoid, but which proved to be great blessings. There is an old Taoist story which I often tell. It offers the wisdom of an old Chinese farmer.

The farmer's horse had run away, and this was a great loss to him, for it was essential to his farm work. A neighbour called in to see him to commiserate. All that the old farmer would say was 'Who knows what is bad and what is good?'

The next day the horse returned, bringing with it a drove of wild horses which it had befriended in its wanderings. The neighbour called again, this time to congratulate him, but the old farmer replied as before, 'Who knows what is bad and what is good?'

The next day, the farmer's son was trying to mount one of the wild horses and he fell off and broke his leg. Once more the neighbour called to commiserate and once more he was met with the same response from the farmer, 'Who knows what is bad and what is good?'

The next day soldiers came to draft able-bodied men into the army, but when they saw the young man with a broken leg, they did not look at him a second time.

There is a ripeness in this philosophy which makes many of our prayers and judgements look superficial. Another assumption we sometimes make is, that having decided what is best for someone, we know also how to attain this. Yet when we look back and trace the sequences of events which led us into what we call tragedy or joy, the most remarkable thing is how small a part we consciously had in them. Great issues appear to have turned upon most trivial things, while carefully laid plans have been tossed aside by factors we could never have foreseen. Our plans may have been thrown upon the dust-heap or turned to ends quite different from those we imagined. The great karmic law is certain. That which is ours must come to us: that which is not ours will pass us by.

So long as we are egotistic enough to assume that we know what is best and how to attain that best, we are in danger. The danger is that we may be tempted to invade the freedom of others by advice or subtle pressure. In this way we can involve ourselves in new karma. We have all come into this life to learn certain lessons, or we should not be here. If a person seeks advice, the wisest thing to say is, 'Have you prayed for guidance to the Father?' 'Have you meditated and asked for direction?' If the enquirer does not know how to set about this, and the matter is urgent, present both sides of the issue impartially, but leave the individual to make up his mind.

If anyone claims that 'the end justifies the means', they are assuming that the end will not change through the particular means used to attain it. This is not necessarily true. The wrong means should not be used to attain the right end, and if they are, the end aimed at will be changed by that fact. How could it ever be supposed that love could be compelled by force, goodness by evil methods, peace achieved through war, or truth supported by falsehood? The karma of the means changes the end.

66

There is much in life that is not easy to accept – indeed that can only be accepted by the growth of trust in God. We must learn to accept death as an experience, while recognising that it is an illusion. It is ironical that transition from a state of more restricted consciousness to one of higher and more extended consciousness should be feared. Yet the task of accepting the transition of someone we love deeply, is a task that is difficult, in spite of faith, trust, knowledge, and some philosophy.

The reason is that our ego is fed constantly in waking life by the senses; so much so that we constantly associate the individual with his physical appearance. What alternative have we? Only an enlightened soul who was constantly familiar with astral levels as well as with the physical one, would find no difficulty. We know intellectually that constant and prolonged grief for a loved one is largely self-pity, yet we go on grieving. At least this shows us our degree of attachment and self-love!

We must also learn to accept incompleteness. As old age comes along, most thoughtful people have a sense that so much has beckoned to them and so little been fulfilled. Opportunities longed for did not come at a time when they could be taken, and perhaps there is a looking back with a sigh. It is important not to overvalue the present life, and to remember that the soul has stored in its treasury the wealth of countless past lives. It may be that the soul requires only some small fragments of experience or one or two lessons to be learned to perfect itself. The conscious part of our mind is in no position to form an assessment of a life's success in terms of what it would like to have attained.

As AE said, 'A man's success or failure is always with his own soul.' Only God can be the judge of this. All that we think of as external is a pale reflection of what is happening on higher interior levels which are participating in the essence of events. G. N. M. Tyrrell expressed this truth when he said, 'The real act of becoming takes place within us, not without.'

If we accept this, our basic attitude towards life should be different from the worldly person's. He evaluates life through his senses: we should ask, 'Am I getting nearer to a consciousness of God?' This is the important question. Reflect upon the tangled skein of human life with its ever-present problems of relationships, jealousies, rivalries, illnesses, accidents (socalled), etc. We are viewing a karmic situation: and life is offering us yet another opportunity to correct our weaknesses, cancels our debts, and strengthen our character. If our surface gaze can see only 'our rights', the ego is once more making a reaction characteristic of its past lives. I should ask myself, 'Am I now prepared to act in the way that love and unselfishness suggest, or shall I allow the ego to direct my actions once more?' A fruitless sequence can be broken once and for all by an act of loving self-negation.

Accept also restriction and limitation. By all means try to change them, but do not resent them. They will change at the right time. In a book called *The Initiate in the New World* a disciple asked his Master to heal him of some disability, and he received this reply: 'When you have learned to ignore it, and work as efficiently as though you hadn't got it, I'll put you on to a cure . . . My son, it is a greater achievement to do good work in spite of a sick body than to cure the body itself.' This is the wisdom of acceptance.

Cultivate love, trust, and humility. This is the third practical suggestion. A master once said, 'Walking along the spiritual path is like walking constantly under an archway of humility with two keys in your hands − the key of love and the key of trust, which will open every door for you.' I shall write very briefly of the first two virtues, humility and love, and concentrate on the third.

Great teachers have all emphasised humility − none more so than Jesus. He said, you will remember, 'Except ye be converted, and become as little children, ye shall not enter into the kingdom of heaven.' He gave an example of this grace to His disciples, just before the Last Supper, when He performed the menial task of washing their feet. Of love I will only say this. It is the paramount virtue and the supreme value. It is a radiation from the soul and has nothing to do with the human emotion. It is strong, kind, tender and enduring, and wants nothing for itself. A sage once wrote of it, 'You live that you may learn to love; you love that you may learn to live. No other lesson is required of man.'

It remains for me before closing this chapter to write something of trust – trust in God. The average human being whose soul is scarcely awake, operates from the ego – a powerful centre built up through hundreds of lives. He calls this 'I'. The ego trusts in wealth, in knowing the right people, in its cunning or experience, in its diplomacy or its influence. It is interesting to observe that three thousand years ago egos were the same. Many phrases in the Old Testament speak of those that 'trust in chariots', they that 'trust in wealth', they that 'trust in graven images', they that trust in 'the Mountain of Samaria'. Translate these into a modern idiom and they apply to modern man. Initiates like David speak of 'trust in the Lord' knowing that everything else men can trust in may let them down. Moses, another great Initiate, four thousand years ago taught the children of Israel in their bitter and desperate desert wanderings, 'The eternal God *is thy* refuge, and underneath *are* the everlasting arms.'

The difference between faith and trust can be simply stated: faith is of the mind, while trust is of the heart. When we apply our minds to a subject and draw conclusions, our attitude may range over a wide scale between conviction and scepticism. The intellect can never achieve certainty – only varying degrees of probability, because all logic overlies certain assumptions which can never be proved. Faith is therefore a willingness to act upon a reasonable belief. Trust does not rely upon the mind's belief, but uses the heart's feeling as its guide.

Job showed this supremely in the midst of all his troubles, when he said, 'Though he slay me, yet will I trust in him.' There is a remarkable story in the Old Testament of three heroic Jews who defied the command of Nebuchadnezzar the Babylonian king, that everyone should worship a particular golden image. As a result of their refusal they were thrown into a furnace but miraculously preserved. Their words to the king illustrate an attitude of complete trust in God. They said, 'We have no need to answer thee in this matter. Our God, Whom we serve is able to deliver us from the burning fiery furnace; and He will deliver us out of thy hand O king. But if not, be it known unto thee, that we will not serve thy gods, nor worship the golden image which thou hast set up.' That the lives of these three men were miraculously preserved, and that they were given high positions in the Province is psychically interesting, but it is not the important thing. It was the spirit of these three men, their trust in God, which is immortal. What should we have done in this situation or its modern equivalent?

Oliver Cromwell is said to have addressed his soldiers, 'Trust in God and keep your powder dry.' The Arabs have a proverb, 'Trust in God and tie the camel's leg.' A contemporary equivalent might be, 'Trust in God and use your common sense', or 'Trust in God and take out a good insurance policy.' Is this trust? If we completely trust God should we be anxious whether our powder is dry or wet? I know that the voice of common sense is saying, 'Is it wrong then to take out a good insurance policy?' 'If I am going into battle, should I be careless as to whether my arms are in a satisfactory condition? Doesn't God expect us to use reasonable prudence and common sense?'

The answer must be I think in terms of our priorities. Trust has to be first. If we are keeping our powder dry because we fear God may let us down, this is not trust. If however our trust is complete we shall not be concerned about the powder we carry. For a pilgrim on the spiritual path there is no half-way house where he can rest satisfied. The more we analyse 'qualified trust' the clearer it is that we cannot serve two masters. Many of us are prepared to trust God so long as things do not depart too much from our wishes.

This attitude implies that we know what is best for us, but we don't! Not one of us knows what is best for the soul. Do we see how the past has been restricted perhaps by one particular weakness which has to be overcome? There is no doubt that so long as we are on earth, our trust will be tested, and it takes a long time before trust comes close to perfection.

A master once put to a group of disciples, 'Suppose you were in a little boat on the open sea with a group of shipwrecked people including those who were dearest to you. Suppose the boat was dangerously full so that to take one more person on board might mean submergence for everyone. Then there arrives at the boat an exhausted swimmer who begs to be taken on board. What would you do?' Some would doubtless use their common-sense and refuse. Others might be prepared to give up their place. No one could actually be sure what he would do until he was actually in that situation. Complete trust implies certainty that whatever happens is in God's hands. The issues of life and death are His.

Either God is wholly trustworthy or not to be trusted at all. There can be no degrees of trust for the pilgrim on the spiritual path. It is all or nothing: this is the goal. Trust is like a seed or acorn which is viable. It has to be sown or it will not grow; and it has to be tended and nurtured or it will die. By no known process can something which is a seed one moment become a full-grown tree the next. We must accept these facts, and all that is expected of us is sincerity, dedication, and genuine effort to live the life that trusts and loves when the going is difficult, recognising that all the difficulties are those we have created for ourselves in the past.

My old friend Ven Sumangalo, a Buddhist priest, told me how on one occasion he found himself in a remote Thai village at the annual fire-walking festival. He watched the headman of the village lead a procession across the hot charcoal beds. After it was completed, he turned to my friend with a gesture which clearly said, 'Will you come too?' My friend described the feelings which surged through him as he realised that if he could not summon up enough courage based upon trust in the Buddha to walk across the fire-beds, he ought to tear up his yellow robes, as being unworthy. The old peasant put out his hand in a friendly gesture, and my friend took it.

He told me that fortunately he recalled that somewhere he had read that if one held on to the hand of a person who had the power, it would protect also the one who trusted. So he went forward, automatically hitching up his cotton robe as he did so. The old peasant said, 'Not necessary'. As my friend was taking the last step on to firm ground, he let go of the hand of the old peasant and unfortunately kicked a hot cinder which landed on the top of one foot. The scar of the burn could be seen there still, he remarked. I asked him later on this question, 'Do you think that in similar circumstances you could do it again?' He wrote back guardedly and said, 'I *think* so.' I did not ask him whether he thought he could do so without the moral support of an outstretched hand. After all, the supporting hand is always God's, whatever inner or outer form it takes.

The only trust that is invulnerable is trust that arises from the soul itself when it hears the voice of God say to the weary pilgrim, 'You can always fall back on Me.' If in the matter of trust we have failed again and again, what does it matter as long as we keep on trying? Only by love and trust in that love, can we come to final truth.

I will write later about cultivating serenity amid the opposites – through non-attachment.

Masters and the Path

In the religious tradition of India and many other Eastern countries, a serious spiritual seeker tries to find someone who is further along the way than he is himself, and asks if he may become his disciple or pupil. The more advanced one is often described as his teacher or guru. This relationship is a fairly common one, and its basis may be one of teaching, advice, example and inspiration, but it is recognised that no teacher can take a pupil beyond the stage he has reached himself. In any case, in spiritual search, intellect cannot take anyone far along the way.

All true spiritual aspirants are mystics and the way is upward and inward towards those higher levels of consciousness beyond mind where things of the spirit are experienced by the soul of man. One of these very high levels of consciousness is called by Hindu mystics, nirvikalpa samadhi, or by Christian mystics illumination or the beatific vision. It is an experience of meeting God – an experience which, if granted on earth in a physical body, enables that soul to close its account with Earth, cast off in succession the restricting bodies, and rise to that level of consciousness which Jesus called the kingdom of God. It, i.e., nirvikalpa samadhi, is a state that cannot be sustained indefinitely, so the mystic falls back to the lower usual level of consciousness.

There are however rare but much higher states of consciousness, one of which is called enlightenment or the spiritual marriage or the unitive life, and in this there is a state of mystical unity with the Divine Being, which is not lost again. These rare beings could truly be called sons of God and could say with Jesus, 'I and my Father are one.' They

73

therefore are expressions in finite form of the Word, or the Christ-consciousness. We may perhaps speculate that in addition to Jesus such sages as Gautama the Buddha, Krishna, Moses, Hermes, Orpheus, Nanak, Kabir, Ramana, and some others may have had this spiritual standing. They are the great ones who have mastered life and return from time to time to help us. It is said that the Earth is never left without some of these great ones upon it. They are all God-conscious or God-realised men, and they are here to do some special work for Him.

There may be many God-conscious beings on earth, but not all of these are masters of the divine path. Some may be powerful beings who have mastered great knowledge and occult power, but they will be reborn because they choose not to be detached from power. I am writing only of masters of the divine path, and for them, the only power they use is love.

A master is consciously and continuously aware of his divine nature, and he can function at will on any level of reality that he chooses, or on all levels simultaneously. He is a finite centre of the Eternal Light, although while on Earth this will be veiled by the bodies he is using. He will look like any other person, and no one would know his status unless he allowed them to know it. The words used in St John's gospel ascribed to Jesus, would be applicable equally to any master. 'I came forth from the Father, and am come into the world: again, I leave the world and go to the Father.' They might be described as brothers of Jesus the Christ – Whom one master described as the Master of masters.

The majority of masters are believed to have reached their high status through age-long effort as human beings. They have trodden the same way as we are treading, aspiring to-wards God. Having reached the kingdom of God, and being free from the wheel, they have nevertheless come back from time to time out of their love and concern for humanity, to help us to travel the same way. According to Indian teaching there are however rare examples of masters who are called Avatars. These are souls specially created by God to embody in finite form as much of the divine spirit as is possible within the limitations of a human body. Avatars have not trodden the long slow way of man's evolution. It may well be that Jesus Christ, Gautama the Buddha, and perhaps others are Avatars in this sense. We shall leave these matters; they are in any case far beyond our capacity to understand with intellect. They are part of the great mysteries.

As we mentioned in the last chapter, incarnate souls who have not yet awakened to the great goal of life which is to return home to God, and be free from the wheel of births and deaths, have before them the long slow process of hundreds of lives with the usual ego-centred outlook. When awakening begins, there is seen on the horizon the great mountain of God, but progress towards it is often slow. There are barren incarnations as well as those which lead the pilgrim-soul nearer to its goal. After endless lives gathering experience some souls reach the foothills of the great mountain.

The tradition is that when six lives have been devoted to this goal, in the seventh life, the soul will be met by a master and offered initiation on the ascending path. If this offer is accepted then the master becomes his guru. The master might say to such a pilgrim, 'I am not here merely to point the way: many others have done this for you in the past. I am here to offer you help, and to give you strength that you will need if you are going to climb this mountain of God. I cannot carry you to the top: it is for you to do the climbing. But I know the path well, as I have been up and down it many times. I shall point out the route, and I shall be with you on the journey. I can give you the strength to reach the mountain-top in one life-time *provided* you will put God absolutely first in your life, and trust me to direct you.'

This is why masters are here on earth. It is a merciful provision of God to make it possible for those who are keen enough to make a special effort to reach the goal, to do so. One thing is quite clear to those souls who have arrived at the mountain-base, that without such divine help it would be quite impossible to reach the summit alone. Mt Everest was a

75

difficult climb, but at last the resources and courage of men proved equal to the task. Of the mountain of God, it can be said without hesitation that no human being could hope to ascend far without a master's help.

It may be asked what happens to those souls who do not make a sufficient effort on the upward climb, or who fail through lack of trust to make the grade while the master is on earth with them? The answer is that they return to the mountain-base, to face the routines of many lives until the time arrives when their master decides again to reincarnate on earth. The once-initiated soul will then be probably called again and once more initiated on to the path up the mountain, thus given another chance to do what he failed to do before. Since masters do not generally return to earth very often, the next opportunity may be perhaps a thousand years later, and after the soul has had many more lives.

It is moving to reflect upon the sacrifice which these great beings make for the sake of helping mankind. Leaving for a time the glory, wonder and freedom of the kingdom, they take upon themselves once more the limitations of the various bodies, subjecting themselves in the process to suffering, tension, treachery, and all that the forces of evil can do to oppose their effort. There is nothing in it for them, but the vast love, the great compassion, the perfect understanding and the fearless courage are Christ-like, and call forth from the heart of one who has been privileged to know one of them, the deepest respect and admiration and love.

Their dearest wish is to take back with them to the kingdom those souls for whom they have accepted responsibility, and who are ready to make the effort required. Few things are more moving than to meditate upon the sacrificial descent of such great souls to help us along. Ramakrishna who died in 1886 developed cancer of the throat; Jesus chose to go to a painful torturing death through crucifixion. Do we reflect that it was not their karma they were discharging, but that of others which they had voluntarily taken over? Thus they gave to others a special opportunity which otherwise they would not have had. The burdens these masters carried were their last bequests to those they loved. They were the wayfarers, the good shepherds, of each of whom it could be said, 'He was bruised for our iniquities; the chastisement of our peace was upon him, and with his stripes we are healed.'

> Beacons of hope, ye appear!
> Languor is not in your heart,
> Weakness is not in your word,
> Weariness not on your brow.
> Ye alight in our van; at your voice,
> Panic, despair, flee away.
> Ye move through the ranks, recall
> The stragglers, refresh the outworn,
> Praise, re-inspire the brave.
> Order, courage, return.
> Eyes rekindling, and prayers,
> Follow your steps as ye go.
> Ye fill up the gaps in our files,
> Strengthen the wavering line,
> Stablish, continue our march
> On, to the bound of the waste
> On, to the City of God.

A master once said to his disciples: 'The only reason you have for this journey is to meet one who can take you home. There are no reasons for sorrow, anxiety, discouragement, or despair. I can take you to the light . . . open the door and let love in.'

I am going to quote from another poet who was sensitive to the heavy load carried by those great servants of humanity. This three-verse poem is entitled *To One Consecrated* and is by the Irish mystic AE.*

> The Mighty Mother made you wise,
> Gave love that clears the hidden ways;
> Her glooms were glory to your eyes,
> Her darkness but the fount of days.

*From *Song and a Fountain* (Macmillan).

She made all gentleness in you
And beauty radiant as the morn's:
She made our joy in yours, then drew
Upon your brow a crown of thorns.

Your eyes are filled with tender light
For those whose eyes are dimmed with tears:
They see your brow is crowned and bright
But not its ring of wounding spears.

A master does the work his Father has given him to do, drawing as little attention to himself as possible. Either he is without ego, or he may retain that perfectly controlled minimum which enables him to discharge what he has come to do. Some esoteric schools (I am thinking more particularly of the Theosophical Society) have spoken of masters as mysterious beings who materialise and dematerialise physical bodies as they will. Olcott's *Old Diary Leaves* and H. P. Blavatsky's books make frequent reference to their personal contacts with the masters Morya, Koot Hoomi, and Dwal Khul whose homes are in Tibet or the near-Himalayan region. I have no reason to doubt these records, but must point out also that great masters have lived among ordinary men and women as householders, in whatever way best assisted their work.

Yogananda's book *Autobiography of a Yogi* gives an account of some of these most remarkable men. We need to remember that the Indian background and tradition is very different from the Western one, in that spiritual aspiration is recognised and understood with sympathy. In our Western setting the same aspiration would be regarded more as a mark of eccentricity or disbalance than of insight and wisdom. Consequently the Eastern master may be well known to those who live around him, and also to devotees far and wide. The Western master finds it expedient to work quietly, secretly and in disguise. Those whose eyes he may have opened are usually required to keep their mouths shut. Those who have no idea they are meeting a master often feel an enormous sense of attraction because of the aura of love and goodness around him; some however tend to move away, as though they are a little fearful, without knowing why. Presumably the evil in them is repelled by the Light.

The masters all teach that seven qualities must become developed by those who aspire to walk along the path of light. These are: love, trust, courage, strength, kindness, tenderness, and humility. The humility of the Western master is often staggering but he is showing through it the lengths to which God will go to bring back lost man to Himself. I often think of those moving lines of Evelyn Underhill's poem *Immanence* –

> I come in little things
> Saith the Lord:
> My starry wings
> I do forsake,
> Love's highway of humility to take:
> Meekly I fit my stature to your need,
> In beggar's part
> About your gates I shall not cease to plead –
> As man, to speak with man –
> Till by such art
> I shall achieve My immemorial plan
> Pass the low lintel of the human heart.

Before any master becomes incarnate, the details of his coming, such as parentage, environment, and timing are carefully selected. Any descent into the realms of mind and matter, which are the domain of the Negative Power, means taking certain risks of karmic involvement. Of course *conscious* knowledge by the incarnating master of his true nature and his mission are inevitably obscure to him during the years of early physical development. This knowledge has to be re-awakened, and therefore some enlightened soul already in a physical body is entrusted with this responsibility. He acts therefore as the guru, until this knowledge becomes fully conscious. Living masters are therefore in a great spiritual succession, and certain sacred symbols and knowledge are handed on like links in a golden chain which bind them into one.

When a master is ready to begin his mission, he will call to him those souls for which he has accepted responsibility, if he sees they are ready to make the effort to climb the mountain of God. A master alone knows who these are. These souls will at the right time hear their master's call, and be brought seemingly by chance, from the ends of the earth if necessary. There is of course no such thing as chance for the human soul. They will be initiated afresh on to the spiritual path up the mountain. This is only done by a master during his earthly life, and there is no justification for supposing that if the path of light is not entered upon here, it can be entered after the death of the physical body. Earthly life is made significant by this fact, and it is of course a school for learning and discipline.

A master is vulnerable until his work here is done. Every master could say, as Jesus once did of His life, 'No man taketh it from me, but I lay it down of myself. I have power to lay it down, and I have power to take it again.' At the same time a master is vulnerable to suffering caused unwittingly by those pupils whom he has accepted and initiated. They have their weaknesses, their failures, their times of doubt and lack of trust, even their treacherous tendencies. The master is like the hub of a wheel, and his initiated pupils are the rim of the wheel. If any part of the rim shows weakness and collapses, the forces of evil seek to enter and undermine the work being done.

These forces may disclose their presence by temporary suffering, illness or even injury to the person of the master. Of course inner resources can be drawn upon by the master and the point of weakness in the rim can be corrected. Those souls whom a master calls to him are supremely fortunate, for they are offered by that act an opportunity which is perhaps the culmination of hundreds of lives. They are offered not the faith and hope of orthodoxy, but knowledge and direction by one who knows, and is a living example of what he teaches. Obedience and trust then become of the highest importance on the part of the pupil. Both will be tested, sometimes severely – but the pupil discovers by experience that everything asked of him is for the evolution of his soul, and the slow destruction of his ego.

The proof of the path's rightness is found in living it. To follow the way pointed out is often far from easy, involving sacrifice and courage, but it is always found in retrospect to have been the right way. By contrast, to diverge and follow the ego's way inevitably leads to trouble and suffering. The master sometimes seems to be leading his pupils along a hard path, but it is for their own good. All their accumulated karma in the current life at least, has to be discharged. Although this experience may seem unduly hard, the counter-blessing is his presence which helps, strengthens, and points the wisest way.

To those who were brought up in the Christian tradition, and listened to exoteric Christianity preached from Sunday pulpits, some of the things stated in this chapter may seem strange, if not unrelated. It is important to remember that there is another esoteric side of Christianity which has never been openly taught, but been confined to mystery schools and small groups which have gathered around a master. In the records of the New Testament it is several times remarked that Jesus spoke to the multitudes in parables, but in private expounded the hidden truth directly to His disciples and the inner circle around Him. The orthodox Christian is disposed to say, 'Why this secrecy? Can spiritual truth do any harm?'

It is an old question and the answer is simple. It is no good teaching a child to run until it can walk. It is no good teaching a schoolboy calculus until his elementary mathematics is sound. If high spiritual truths were taught before basic ones were mastered it would be utterly discouraging and might set back the hearer for many lives. An orthodox person may say, 'If I have surrendered my life to Jesus Christ and am trying to practise the things He taught, why should I need a living master? Have I not got one?' To this I should simply reply,

'If this is how you feel, and you keep on walking with sincerity, courage and persistence, you will reach the foothills in due course.' But when you stand at the foot of the great mountain of God you will recognise – as every other person who has stood there has done – that you can only ascend with the help of a living guide.

If such a one offers you help then, you will know he is a messenger from God. Such messengers or masters came from the kingdom, assuming a human body in order to do work that could not be done from higher levels. A master inspires, offers constant help and strength, reproves where necessary, tests his pupils for their trust, watches their reactions, indicates the danger points, and does all this out of love for their souls. This intimate relationship is essential to progress.

May I say to the orthodox that Jesus Christ Himself never claimed to be the 'only-begotten' Son of God. This claim was made later by the Church's theologians. All true masters who have reached the higher samadhi can rightly be called sons of God, for each of them expresses in a finite form something of the Divine Being. Rightly understood they may all therefore be expressions of the Christ-consciousness. Jesus did say, 'I *am* in the Father, and the Father in me.' Kabir said, 'Listen my brother! The Lord who ravishes my eyes has united Himself with me.'

Nanak said, 'The steward of God becomes God Himself; do not be deceived by his human body.'

I think Ramana Maharshi's words sum things up, and might well be studied by those who like to argue about such things. He said:

'So long as duality persists in you, the Guru is necessary. Because you identify yourself with the body, you think the Guru too is the body. You are not the body, nor is the Guru. You are the Self, and so is the Guru . . . But as long as you think you are separate, or that you are the body, so long is the outer Master necessary, and He will appear as if with a body.'

I turn now to a question often asked, 'How can one find a

master?' I have suggested already that the Eastern and Western environments are in this respect quite different. Dr Julian Johnson makes no secret of his seven years' stay at Radha Soami Sat Sang in Beas, Punjab. He has written several books about his time there. Yet even in India many masters prefer to work quietly and unknown. In the Western world to set out in search of a master would probably be futile. How could one recognise such a one? No true master would make any claim to be such. If he made any public admission it might be to say that he was a servant of God. But it is equally likely that he might be facetious or deliberately misleading to a persistent questioner, and the latter might be told that his questioning was unethical and improper. Certainly no one could know a master's status unless the latter allowed him to know it. The process would be a lifting of the consciousness of the enquirer, so that he *knew*, but he would not know how he knew.

There is an interesting passage in the 11th chapter of the *Gita* where the divine Krishna is talking to Arjuna (an awakening disciple). Arjuna begs his Master to allow him a vision of Him in his divine form. At first amazed and afterwards terrified and overwhelmed, Arjuna then begs Lord Krishna 'Please take again the form I knew. Be merciful O Lord, Thou who art the Home of the whole Universe.' Then Arjuna offers to Him a moving prayer, such as every disciple of a master must at times have felt like offering. 'Whatever I have said to Thee in rashness, taking Thee only for a friend . . . and addressing Thee in thoughtless familiarity, not understanding Thy greatness; whatever insult I have offered to Thee in jest, in sport or in repose, in conversation or at banquet, alone or in a multitude, I ask Thy forgiveness for them all. O Thou who art without an equal.'

A master will usually say to a disciple seeking for a more personal relationship, 'I am your teacher first, and then your friend. I am not interested in your personalities: I am concerned only for your souls.'

The right answer therefore to the question, 'How can I find

a master?' is – in the Western world – 'You can't!' If you are destined by your life's pattern to meet a master, you can be quite certain that everything that is necessary to that end will come about. But one cannot manipulate the pattern or introduce what is not already there.

There is a remaining question likely to be asked, 'What is meant by initiation?' It is a question I shall only attempt to answer in very general terms. This event is the greatest one which has happened to a soul since it was first created. What happens is not visible from the outside, but is concerned with the soul. An unconscious link between the soul and its master is confirmed consciously.

The master takes over the responsibility for leading and guiding the soul up the mountain of God to the very top, while the pupil gratefully accepts the master's direction and promises to put God absolutely first in his life. The relationship is a close one on interior levels, and the pupil, wherever he is, is being observed and assessed. The pupil learns by experience that he will never be compelled to do anything or go anywhere, but that if he goes the way which is suggested to him, it will prove the best. For many pupils the learning of obedience is not an easy thing, for through countless lives past the ego has gone its own way.

The essence of spiritual growth involves the wearing away of this ego in order that the soul may grow and rule the life. After initiation, a master may decide to take charge of the karma of that pupil in order to give the soul an opportunity to reach the mountain-top in this life. Normally for the uninitiated person, the karma of the past which has to be met will be spread over several lives, but with initiation this will require that karma may have to come thick and fast. It is, so to speak, concertinard. If this situation is considered, it will be clear that walking on this path involves courage, patience, great trust in the teacher, great strength of purpose and great humility.

These things will be achieved if the love for the teacher is great enough. The pupil has of course to make a considerable effort – even a supreme effort – although he is free to climb, to linger, or to turn back. If he gives up the effort he will have to wait for another life, and it might be a wait of one or two thousand years before his master is once more in human form on this planet. It is likely that he will then be called to face the task he shirked before, but as the pupil will probably have built up more karma in the lives he has lived between, his task may not be easier but harder.

For a pupil who takes his opportunity seriously, life will now be a struggle between his ego and his soul. The ego will fight with every resource to keep its rulership. It is the old lower self built up through the past lives, and it keeps the soul imprisoned. The master watches all this, but the pupil is not obliged to go in the way suggested, and will probably then be faced with learning through suffering. To become the pupil of a living master is the greatest of human privileges, and every soul will have this opportunity in due course, if it yearns for it. Let us wipe out of our minds the false idea that some souls will be saved and others lost.

A great master once said, 'Every soul is saved.' But as a rosebud cannot be compelled to open before its time, souls are given freedom to germinate or remain latent according to their choice. To be called by a living master does not mean that such a soul is any more advanced than others, but it means that its master is at that time in a physical body on Earth and sees that the time has arrived for the pupil to make a special effort.

In the previous chapter on *The Soul's Great Journey* I wrote that when the soul is tired enough of the far country and wants to return to the kingdom, it might practise four courses of action to lead it on the way. They will be essential practices once initiated, so if they are cultivated now, they must lead to the mountain-foot and ultimately to the Master Himself. I spoke of the first three. The first was constantly watching the antics of the ego-self. The second was learning acceptance of life rather than showing constant resentment. The third was to cultivate the three golden virtues of humility, love and trust. The fourth, which I left until today was to cultivate serenity amid the opposites through non-attachment. In simple terms to stop wanting things for yourself.

The call to stop wanting is definitely at variance with the Western attitude to life. Most persons want things, or persons, for themselves; or they want position, influence, fame or importance, power and wealth – the baubles of our civilisation. This is the world of *desire* which all the sages have told us can offer no permanent satisfaction. Everything that is acquired can subsequently be lost. The Buddha particularly stressed this 2,500 years ago. He told men that human life was riddled with suffering and that desire was the cause of it.

Desire resulted in attachment to finite things and persons, and when these were lost or taken away then suffering resulted. Desire itself brings men back to birth again. The Buddha's attitude is perfectly illustrated by a story which is told of Him. There came one day to consult Him a business man of great wealth and also well known for his philanthropy. He asked the Buddha whether he would not be making better use of his life if he wound up his affairs, gave his wealth away, and adopted the yellow robe of a disciple. Seeing that he was perfectly sincere, the Buddha said to him,

'He that is attached to wealth had better cast it away than allow his heart to be poisoned by it, but he who does not cleave to wealth, and who, possessing riches uses them rightly, will be a blessing to his fellow men. I say to thee remain in thy station in life and give thyself with diligence to thy enterprises. It is not life and wealth and power that enslave men, but their attachment to life and wealth and power.'

In the *Bhagavad Gita* Krishna has much to say about desire and attachment. A few typical sentences will show this.

'Desire consumes and corrupts everything. It is a man's greatest enemy. As fire is enshrouded in smoke, a mirror by dust, and a child by the womb, so is the universe enveloped in desire. It is the wise man's constant enemy, it tarnishes the face of wisdom. It is as insatiable as a flame of fire. Therefore O Arjuna, first control thy senses and then slay desire.'

Here are another two sentences:

'The soul that moves in the world of the senses, and yet keeps the senses in harmony, free from attraction and aversion, finds rest in quietness. In this quietness falls down the burden of all her sorrows, for when the heart has found quietness, wisdom has also found peace.'

Similar teaching was given by Jesus when He said, 'Lay up for yourself treasures in heaven . . . for where your treasure is, there will your heart be also.' One final saying about non-attachment is that of Akbar the Mogul emperor, well known for his appreciation of all religious faiths. He said, 'The world is a bridge: pass over it but build no house upon it.' All the sages point to the wisdom of non-attachment if we are to live at peace within the opposites. It is a razor-edged path that we are called upon to walk between the slope of withdrawal from the world and involvement with the world. The characteristic Indian tendency in the past has been towards withdrawal, and the characteristic Western tendency has been towards involvement. One might perhaps summarise the advice of the sages as, 'Know the world for what it is; use it, and serve God in it, but don't let desires anchor you to it.' Since it is a razor-edged path we shall examine it more closely.

First, let us be clear that non-attachment is not the same as indifference. Of course it is true that a person who is indifferent to things or persons is not attached to them. But this is not the non-attachment of which the sages speak. It includes appreciation. The attitude of Jesus showed appreciation of nature and of people around Him. He appreciated the simplicities and beauty of life, the birds of the air, the grass of the fields, the ordinary tasks of the sower and reaper and the homely housewife. He was however non-attached, and the evidence is that· when the time came to say farewell to them, He did so without hesitation or suffering at having to part with them. It is not appreciation which is undesirable but the emotional attitude of attachment. The test is simple – would I feel suffering if they were taken from me?

Let me touch briefly on attachment to persons. Is it possible to be non-attached to persons whom you deeply love? From the familiar human viewpoint this would be called indifference: but is this necessarily so? This raises the nature of love between say, parent and child, husband and wife, between lovers, and between friend and friend. Human love may range between something noble and sacrificial on the one hand, and the degradation of lust on the other extreme.

Human love always has some finite person to whom it is directed. The bond may be strong and subtle but almost always involves the emotion of desire. It is wanting someone for one's self. If by contrast, we look at divine love, this is a spiritual radiation. It is non-attached because it is unlimited: it is not concentrated exclusively on one person, and in this sense it is impersonal. It remains the same even when there is no response on the part of the one who is loved. We must face the truth that even noble and sacrificial human love *wants* some response, and if this is not finally forthcoming it tends to wilt and die. Divine love is unchanging and does not pass away. The test therefore of non-attached love is: do I want or expect anything for myself from it?

Someone may ask, 'Then is human love wrong? Can I not love another person for his or her sake?' The answer is that there is no right or wrong here. We all do love in the human way, and must recognise that we sow the seeds of sorrow by doing so. Human love is never wholly unselfish, for it gains something from it – if only the sense for the time being of wholeness or completeness. In pure divine love flowing through a human soul there is a constancy that needs no response for its preservation, and it irradiates with its warmth all who are in the path of its flowing. I think this high teaching was understood by William Blake the mystic who wrote:

> He who binds to himself a Joy
> Doth the winged life destroy;
> But he who kisses the Joy as it flies
> lives in Eternity's sunrise.

Our task on the path is to purify our love from its limitations and selfishness, and open ourselves to the divine quality of love. Jesus said to His disciples in His few closing words to them, 'A new commandment I give unto you, That ye love one another; as I have loved you.' This statement clearly inspired these two fine verses of Horatius Bonar:

> Beloved, let us love;
> Love is of God;
> In God alone hath love
> Its true abode.
>
> Beloved, let us love:
> For only thus
> Shall we behold that God
> Who loveth us.

The Nature and Problem of Time

A well-known astronomer, the late A. S. Eddington of Cambridge, once wrote: 'In any attempt to bridge the domains of expeience belonging to the spiritual and physical sides of our nature, time occupies the key position.' This statement is justification enough for this chapter. Alongside of it I want to place a sentence of a very well-known philosopher A. N. Whitehead, 'It is impossible to meditate upon time, and the mystery of the creative passage of nature, without an overwhelming emotion at the limitations of human intelligence.'

We are all subject to change, and change leads us back to this mystery of time. When the intellect has made its greatest effort it has done no more than lift the corner of the encompassing veil. The mystery remains, and we can only fall on our knees and pray from the centre of our being, 'O Thou, Who changest not, abide with me.'

I find my 'overwhelming emotion' is not so much associated with 'the limitations of human intelligence' for I have long had no illusions about this. My emotion is because so many hearts are torn and lacerated by time, until the light of the soul's knowledge of eternity touches them. Let me illustrate.

I recall a few sentences of Hugh Walpole the English novelist. He was facing a critical moment of life when death seemed imminent and certain. Reflecting on it afterwards he said, 'I remember feeling sorry . . . that I must leave two people whom I dearly loved, but most of all that I must abandon so many beautiful things, tiny things: the sound of running water, birch trees in the sun, a hot day by the sea,

90

music, reading a good book by the fire, a walk over the hills, and so on. Then, *with absolute conviction*, I was aware that whatever I had found lovely and of good report, I should still enjoy.' Happily the soul's knowledge shone through the storm-clouds of life for Walpole, but for how many of the Earth's millions would this be true?

Let us consider first a few commonplace observations which we have all made about time. Space and time are unlike anything else that we experience. We cannot see, hear, taste, touch or smell them. Yet without them we should possess no senses at all. They seem to have no beginning and no end: yet even to say this, shows how conditioned our minds are. It is difficult to imagine ourselves not in space and not in time. It is commonplace to hear people say time heals, and time offers another chance, yet at other times we hear that time is a deceiver and a destroyer. We talk about saving time, about wasting time, about not having enough time: but we have all the time there is!

Time has been described as like a refreshing river, an ever-rolling stream, a bird on the wing, a winged chariot, and so on – all of which have, in common, movement in one direction. If we think time flows, it is we who are stationary – but might not time be stationary and we be moving through time? In common speech we talk of past, present, and future, but do these correspond to anything real or are they divisions of convenience like lines of latitude and longitude? The present moment which we call 'now' is a vanishingly small interval of time wedged between the past and future. In theory it has no extension at all, yet it is the one bit of time in which we can gather knowledge or act in the world. We cannot hang on to the present: if we try to do this it has already become the past and a portion of the future has moved in to become the present.

It is as though each individual is like a wheel running along a rail called time. The contact of the wheel with the rail is in theory a one-point contact, but it sustains the whole weight of our life. Because this present moment is so important to us

91

it is regarded as a very small but definite time interval, and it is called the 'specious present'.

It is strange also to reflect that the present moment which we call 'now' is not likely to be identical with the 'now' of persons on other planets or stars. If we tried to arrange this we could not do so, for it would have to be attempted by light signals, and light takes a finite time to travel. Light takes 1.3 seconds to reach us from the moon, 8 minutes from the sun, 4½ years from the nearest star, 2 million years from the nearest galaxy, and so forth. The strange deduction follows that when we look up at the night sky, the pattern does not correspond to anything that exists *now*, but we see each object where it was and as it was at different times in the past. I shall not speak of Einstein's views because they are too difficult for the non-specialist to appreciate.

I shall however mention a distinction which psychologists make between clock-time which is common to everyone and used in practice, and the concept of psychological time – which is subjective – and peculiar to the individual and his mood. We have all remarked that time seems to pass quickly if our interest is deeply involved, and slowly if we are bored. Thus it passes quickly for a mathematician solving a fascinating problem; for a person watching an exciting film, or for two lovers deeply interested in each other. It passes slowly if we are thirsty and waiting for the kettle to boil, if we are under strain or anxiety. The subjective sense of the passage of time seems to vary very much with the emotional content of the mind: but there seems no simple way of correlating clock-time and psychological time.

Now I want to mention some less familiar phenomena associated with time. Here is one which is little known, and not understood. If you hypnotise a person and, for example, say, 'In 2 hours 37 minutes from now, you will sit down and write me a letter stating what time you believe it to be when you start to write,' this direction will be carried out with considerable accuracy in relation to the sense of time passing. Of course, the person is awakened after the suggestion is made, but kept away from clocks, watches, radio, etc. or any ordinary means of knowing how time is going. It would appear that there is some inner monitor in the mind of man closely linked with time.

The action of hallucinogenic drugs has a bearing on the mind's link with time. Some years ago a British member of Parliament wrote about his experiences under mescalin. He reported that he was able to experience events not merely in their normal time sequence, but also out of their correct order. For example, a tea-trolley was wheeled in, and he re-marked that this event could be observed a number of times with interpolations from other parts of time in between. As time passed however he noted that the interpolations were fewer, i.e., the tea-trolley events persisted – and from this he surmised he was back in a normal observing state.

Then at the peak of the drug's activity he noticed that at intervals he became unaware of his surroundings, and was conscious of himself in 'a state of breathless wonderment and complete bliss' for what he took to be long intervals of time. These intervals could only have been short because he was being given simple intelligence test questions, and the absence of response would have been obvious. He said however that for some days he remembered that afternoon not as so many hours spent in the sitting room interrupted by these strange excursions, but as countless years of complete bliss interrupted by short spells in the sitting room. He also said, 'During this period I would be aware of a pervasive, bright, pure light, like a kind of invisible sunlit snow.' This strongly suggests the Light to which mystics refer in high states of consciousness close to Illumination.

Side by side with these observations I place some by R. H. Ward, a distinguished English writer. Under the influence of L.S.D. taken under medical supervision, he observed his hand apparently growing smaller, until it became the size of an infant's hand. He became afraid that this might go on indefinitely and lead to his extinction. This led him to struggle out of the experience. His later comments are interesting. He says that on the diminished hand he noticed a scar which in reality had been caused only a week ago. Ward remarks pertinently, 'So when one was a child, this scar was already there, just as now; when one is a man one's childhood hand, like all of everything else, is still there. Yes, all time is one time!'

Ward made another observation when looking at his face in a mirror at the height of the experiment. He observed his face changing – going backwards in time to become like that of a small boy with the bright hair, eyes and cheeks of childhood, while simultaneously he saw his face changing into that of an old white-haired man, thin-lipped and wrinkled, with bones prominent beneath the skin, eyes sunken and veins blue on the temple. The present image was there, concurrently with the other two. He comments provocatively, 'These movements in opposite directions were really one movement in a direction unknown to us – a dimension to which our consciousness is a stranger.'

Now I want to mention two remarkable phenomena associated with time. If you go back into antiquity you will always find records of the belief in soothsayers, auguries, prophets, fortune-tellers, etc. i.e., of persons who are able to obtain knowledge of events still in the future, which later come to pass. During this century a great deal of work has been done on this phenomenon, now called precognition. I quote briefly the views of three authorities in this field.

H. F. Saltmarsh was a trusted officer of the London Society for Psychical Research and sifted their large collection of evidential data. He wrote, 'After prolonged study, I have no hesitation in affirming that precognitions do occur. In doing so I have the support of many authorities in psychical research.'

Professor Bozzano examined a thousand records and set aside all those which could possibly be interpreted as due to self-suggestion or the use of any other paranormal faculties. He reported that there remained a solid core of cases which could not be explained in any other way than the recognizing of precognition.

Professor Charles Richet, a physiologist in the University of Paris, who died in 1935, was a Nobel prizeman and a careful observer. When he was convinced by observational data, it was known that they were reliable data. For many years he was deeply interested in psychical research, and stated that he was convinced of what today we would call E.S.P. – embracing telepathy, clairvoyance, precognition, etc. He also stated that he was convinced of tele-kinesis – the same term as our psycho-kinesis. Thirdly, he said he was convinced of the appearance of ectoplasm in materialisation phenomena. He was well aware that these facts would not fit into the limited orthodox scientific picture of the world, and he was oppressed by a sense of our abysmal ignorance. He said, 'Precognition is a demonstrated verity. It is a strange, paradoxical, and seemingly absurd fact, but one that we are compelled to admit . . . The explanation will come (or will not come) later. The facts are none the less authentic and reliable.'

Let us turn now to retrocognition, which is the term used for 'seeing into the past' – to put it popularly. Precognition has always aroused more interest than retrocognition. Precognition *seems* more mysterious. It admittedly does raise difficulties with our notions of causation and freewill. Since people are all familiar with memory as a function of normal mind, I think they feel that retrocognition is the sort of thing we might expect by adopting an extended view of memory. Thus for example, if the etheric prototype of a place could hold a memory, in the sense of retaining impressions of events which have taken place there, a sensitive person coming into that locality might pick them up.

This hypothesis has been used to explain hauntings, object-reading and so on. On this view there is preserved a kind of cosmic memory-record of all that takes place on the lower levels: it has been called the akashic record by some occult schools. There are some notable cases of retrocognition of which I will mention (for lack of space) only one. Miss Moberly and Miss Jourdain were distinguished academic figures who visited the Petit Trianon at Versailles in 1901 and both of them had experiences which led them to believe that they had seen it as it was in the time of Marie Antoinette, a century before. Their observations were of a 'live' sense, and the information was afterwards confirmed by researches undertaken into French National Archives.

In what terms can we start to understand these many strange phenomena linked with time? Let us dismiss without further ado the crude popular idea that the past is done with, the present moment is being created, and the future is blank. On such a view there is no accounting for non-inferential pre-cognition, for there is nothing there to see, if the future is blank! The alternative possibility is that all things that ever were, are, or will be, are in existence always. All that an individual does is to come across them, one at a time.

Figure 3 illustrates this viewpoint, in which the events

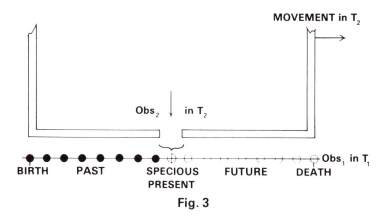

Fig. 3

which constitute a person's life are presented as beads on a string. There is a screen with a slot in it, and the observer behind this screen cannot see the whole series of life-events, but only meets them one at a time as the moving slot discloses them to him. The width of this slot is called the specious present, and it represents a very small time-interval wedged in

96

between past and future. Observer 1 is the physical aspect of the person, while Observer 2 in the moving box is essentially the mind-aspect of the person. Notice that since we have treated Time 1 as though it were a dimension of space, we must have another dimension of time, called Time 2 to account for the movement of the slot over Time 1.

This outlook has something to commend it, for since the future is filled with events still to be experienced, their existence provides a basis for precognition. The question now is 'How can they be foreseen?' To make the problem as simple as possible let us take an example:

'A mother dreamed that she had been followed by a monkey and, having an aversion to monkeys, she came down to breakfast rather upset and related the dream to her husband at the breakfast table. He suggested that she should take the children out for a walk in order to throw off the unpleasant dream-atmosphere. When she did this, in the streets of London, she was followed by a monkey which she described later as 'the very monkey of my dream'.

Assume this to be a precognitive dream. It is non-inferential, for there were no previous observations which record the frequency of appearance of monkeys in the streets of London. I am sure you would not be willing to suppose that the mother's dream caused the monkey to walk in the streets of London some hours later, nor would you find it easy to suppose that the walking monkey caused the mother's dream some hours earlier – for this would reverse the arrow of causation. If the two events – the walking monkey and the mother's dream are not related as cause and effect, how are they related?

To account for this we must bring in the structure of man as shown in Fig. 1 with his many levels. This structure of man is combined with Fig. 3 to make Fig. 4, but an important new idea has been introduced in Fig. 4: this is due to Saltmarsh, and it is that the specious present widens out considerably on higher levels of the self. It might for example, be a few minutes on the etheric level; it might be hours on the astral levels; it might be months on the mental levels; years wide on the causal level and even millenia wide on the spiritual level. Note that the precognition is a mental event. In the above case it was a dream, but it might have been a vision, or a communication through automatic writing, or by any means which the unconscious may use to exteriorise its knowledge. Its precognitive character is not known until the physical event which fulfils it is experienced.

Now let us see how the concepts of Fig. 4 account for the phenomena of time.

If we had a world which was wholly physical, we could account for physical events happening in that world by Fig. 3. The time-dimension T_1 is called duration, and the time-dimension T_2 is called succession. Obs_1 is the physical body and Obs_2 the mental structure. The arrow of causation points along the direction of movement in T_2, i.e. from what we call past to future. We assume that the earlier events cause the later ones.

Figure 4 brings in the detailed structure of man. His causal level is, among many other things, the karmic storehouse linking his succession of lives together, and from this level the karmic seeds of events which are to come are precipitated when 'ripe'. They fall slowly downwards through the levels of diminishing reality. These seeds of thought are malleable or plastic at an early stage of their fall, but become less so as they descend, and are fixed in form when they touch the present moment of the physical level and are experienced by the senses.

Suppose X_2 is an event seen in a dream and suspected of being a precognition. It is in the future so far as the brain level is concerned, but it may later be identified with the physical event X_1 which happens later. This precipitation of karmic thought-seeds from the causal level downwards is at the basis of each human life, so that the fundamental arrow of causation is downwards, *from above to below* (not from left to right), as we assume because we identify ourselves with our bodies. I have marked this arrow T_3.

I think (but am not certain) that this is a third dimension of time. From above to below is a direction of diminishing reality. Expressing it the other way round: from below to above is the direction of increasing reality with which we become familiar in meditation. T_3 is the representative in the region of mind of something we call eternity on the levels of spirit.

If you look at Fig. 4 again, you see that the widening specious present as we ascend makes it possible to cognise future possible events, as we lift our consciousness. What we precognise normally, is not a future which *must* be but one which will be if no new factors enter in. Such new factors as prayers, changed attitudes, or the intervention of higher beings who can operate with their minds on a high level in a wide specious present. It seems to me that the whole of the dotted region is one in which new factors are frequently operative to change karmic events as they are precipitated. Take the following example:

Mrs W was staying with her little daughter Margaret and a nursemaid near Edinburgh. She writes:

'Between 3 and 4 o'clock I told little Margaret to go outside and play in the railway garden. This was a strip of ground between the sea-wall and the railway embankment, which was closed by a gate at each end. After a few minutes, I heard a voice, as it were within me, saying – "Send for her back, or something dreadful will happen to her." At the same time I was seized with terror and trembling. At last I rose hastily and asked the nursemaid to go and bring little Margaret home. During this period of absence the terror increased, so that I feared I should never see the child alive again. About a quarter of an hour later the servant returned with her safe and well . . . later that afternoon an engine and tender jumped the rails, broke through the protecting wall and crashed on to the rocks where Margaret had been intending to play. Three men out of five were killed.'

It seems clear that Mrs W had enough psychic sensitivity to

be aware of some menacing event drawing nearer, but not enough to know what was its nature. She felt it concerned Margaret, and by sending for her to return home, she frustrated what would otherwise have been a tragedy for the little girl. That Mrs W's intense anxiety arose from a genuine precognition is shown here by a sufficient part of the event being unchanged, resulting in the deaths of three others.

Let us now look at the strange phenomena of time disclosed under the influence of psychedelic drugs. Mayhew said that he experienced events 'out of their true time-order, and also the same event more than once'. If his consciousness was lifted to a high level of mind where the specious present was of a few hours' duration, he would be able to see the events of the afternoon as many times as he cared to and also in any time order . . . He had only to move the focus of his attention in his wide specious present.

He observed also that he was 'at intervals unaware of his surroundings, in a state of breathless wonderment and complete bliss', and this could be interpreted as his consciousness fluctuating up and down along T_3. His recollection of the afternoon's experience as 'countless years of pure bliss interrupted by short spells in the drawing room' is consistent with the statements of many mystics that 'time didn't seem to exist'. This refers to T_2 in particular since change would be unnoticed as long as their focus of awareness was away from the two ends of their specious present. If they looked at their past edge, events would be seen disappearing, while at the future edge new events would be slowly appearing.

Mr Ward's observation of his face viewed in a mirror, is clearly a view of Obs_1 which could only be made when the specious present was wide enough to embrace the greater part of the life-span. This would be a high level of T_3. To use an analogy, we do not need to run from one end of a queue to the other to appreciate its length: it is sufficient to move a short distance away from the queue, but at right angles to it.

We can ask innumerable questions about time, but we can offer few intelligible answers. If we ask 'To what does the restrictive slot in Figs. 3 and 4 correspond in the region of mind' we cannot say. We notice that on the physical level the restriction of time in a specious present is greatest, while on the level of spirit there is virtually no restriction (so that T_2 is meaningless). Everything just *is*.

Similarly we recognise that spatial restriction in form, i.e., the isolation and separateness of individuals is most marked on the physical level, while on the higher levels mystics speak of the great inter-relatedness and unity of everything. The restrictions which we suffer in both space and time seem designed to assist the maturing of consciousness in the soul. Unless we first experienced the restrictions of time and space, how could we appreciate the eternal and the infinite? Unless we suffered the unreal, how could we know the real? This points to the limitations of man's lot as a provision of the All-Compassionate One to allow us, *if we will*, to know Him.

I found one of the most intriguing remarks of Mr Ward was where he speaks of 'an absolute presence of bliss' and says also 'the sense of rightness and inevitability was immeasurably enhanced . . . and so was the sense of familiarity – this was something one remembered'. This suggests the territory of the soul itself – the very heights of being. Did the soul remember its first creation – when the sons of God shouted for joy because these new creations of God were capable after their long journey through time and unreality of returning also as sons?

Meditating upon Fig. 4 I make an outrageous speculation. We know that on the basis of a supposed precognition action can be taken which will modify or change the otherwise probable future. In retro-cognition events can be seen in a wide specious present also. Then could not action be taken to modify that past event? If it could, I do not know what consequences might follow. Perhaps the speculation is however not utterly foolish for a statement made by a recent communicator from the other side is as follows:

'I can't prophesy because things depend upon many human imponderables. And yet there is the miracle that

101

events in time can be modified and altered both backwards and forwards *outside time.*

One of the wider questions relevant to precognition which is sometimes asked is, 'Why is the particular selection of facts precognised? Out of ten thousand possibilities, why were these singled out?' Of course if the precognition is of a warning nature it is sufficient to suggest that the soul, which knows the life-pattern, will choose the material which would be most effective to stimulate action. Not all precognitive glimpses are of a warning nature, so our question remains.

The late Miss Graham Ikin suggested that some precognitions are to reassure the recipient that when they are experienced on the physical level, it was a situation which the soul had foreseen as being essentially right and conforming to the divine life-pattern. I am sure this is true. Miss Ikin gives a personal illustration.

An earlier precognitive glimpse was fulfilled for her when she was in a nursing home in Liverpool in 1930. She writes of this nursing home experience:

> 'It looked as though my going there had been a mistake, and yet I could not get away. Then, one day, the nurse turned the mirror at the back of the dressing table round, so that I could see the street through it (from my bed), and *through that mirror* I saw the scene that had been precognised long before. I knew that though everything in me wanted to get away, that was where I was meant to be. The results justified it subsequently.'

If I may comment it would be to say that this seems to me an example of that everlasting mercy which so often cushions for us the very hard situations of life, virtually saying, 'Don't be troubled; accept this as a part of the great pattern which you have to meet.'

One of the obvious and difficult questions that is rightly raised is 'How far are we free?' Is the view of time which we have presented, consistent with a belief in freewill? If we were

102

dealing with a purely physical world, I have no doubt that determinism would reign: there would be no freedom. But the physical level that we know and participate in is inter-penetrated by mind and influences from higher levels still, so there is not complete determinism. At the other extreme, the light within the soul of man is divine and completely free. As we descend through the various levels of reality the amount of freedom diminishes and of determinism grows.

Since every individual is a complex being participating in many levels, we cannot give a simple answer to the question of freedom. The higher levels of ourselves, even though im-mature as yet do have some freedom. In particular they can choose how they will react to circumstances and events. The physical level is to a large degree the product of karma: we created it ourselves in our past lives. But since the lower planes into which the soul descends are here in the interests of the soul's growth, our present reactions affect our future karma. Are we courageous in the face of adversity? Do we trust God when things appear to be going against us? It is largely in the quality of response to events that our freedom lies.

Freedom is something we can win – or fail to win – for ourselves. The sage and mystic is able to influence events considerably. Some events in the pattern of life are doubtless inescapable, some are probabilities and still others we may modify partially or completely. The mother who heard a voice saying, 'Send for your little daughter or something dreadful will happen to her', had won enough freedom to sense impending danger, but not enough to know what it was. She was able to intervene to save her child's life. If she had been a very advanced soul she would have known the nature of the coming event, and doubtless been able to prevent the engine from jumping the rails.

Let us attempt a summing up of our views of time. Observer₁ is physical or the least real part of us and ends his existence with physical death. His experience in regard to mental and emotional characteristics has been shared with

103

Obs_2. Obs_2 survives the event of physical death and continues his life in T_2 and T_3. T_2 is essentially time as the mind knows it, and accounts for change, but it becomes of diminishing significance as we climb through the levels of increasing reality and find the specious present greatly extending. T_3 points us to the direction of increasing reality. It is only dominant for us in moments of mystical perception – and then it is Obs_3 – the soul which is the observer. Of T_3 we might say in the words of William Blake, 'Time is the mercy of eternity'.

It is all we can hope to know of eternity on these lower levels. To be conscious of being Obs_3 and thus to experience T_3 is to be a mystic. We then *know* that all things are working together for good. We do not need to escape from T_1 and T_2 to discover T_3: we are always in it although not consciously so. I do not think man should pray for the presence of God: this has never left him, for it is the light within the soul, but he should pray for greater purity of heart and life so that he may become increasingly sensitive to this presence.

The whole pageant of human life is a poignant spectacle. The planet has seen great civilisations rise and fall. The process is still going on, although the trends are not always easy to recognise when one is in the midst of them. I do not find profound meanings in history – only lessons that men are slow to learn. It seems to me the reflection on a large scale of the slow progress of the human heart to recognise things that are beyond time. In this pageant, a man's life is no more than a single day at school.

It seems to me that to know oneself – the soul – in T_3 (the eternal dimension) is the aspiration of the mystics about which I shall write in the next chapter. I was very interested to find two examples in literature of this perception, and I shall present these before closing.

The first is taken from J. B. Priestley's autobiographical book *Rain upon Godshill*.

He describes it as a dream which he had. Its symbolism probably arises from the activity of bird-ringing with which

104

he had been recently helping at St Catherine's lighthouse in the Isle of Wight.

'I dreamed I was standing at the top of a very high tower alone, looking down upon myriads of birds, all flying in one direction. Every kind of bird was there . . . It was a noble sight, this vast aerial river of birds. But now time was speeded up so that I saw generations of birds, watched them break their shells, flutter into life, weaken, falter, and die. Wings grew only to crumble; bodies were sleek, and then in a flash, bled and shrivelled, and death struck everywhere at every second. What was the use of all this blind struggle towards life, this eager trying of wings, all this gigantic meaningless biological effort? As I stared down, seeming to see every creature's ignoble little history almost at a glance, I felt sick at heart. It would be better if not one of them, not one of us all, had been born − if the struggle ceased for ever. I stood on my tower, still alone, desperately unhappy. But now the gear was changed again . . . time went faster still, and it was rushing past at such a rate that the birds could not show any movement, but were like an enormous plain sown with feathers. But along this plain, flickering through the bodies themselves, there now passed a sort of white flame, trembling, dancing, then hurrying on; and as soon as I saw it, I knew that this flame was life itself, the very quintessence of being.

'Then it came to me in a rocket-burst of ecstasy that nothing mattered, nothing could ever matter, because nothing else was real but this quivering and hurrying lambency of being. Birds, men or creatures, not yet shaped or coloured, all were of no account except in so far as this flame of life travelled through them. It left nothing to mourn over behind it. What I had thought was tragedy was mere emptiness or a shadow; for now all real feeling was caught and purified and danced on ecstatically with the white flame of life. I had never before felt such deep happiness as I knew at the end of my dream of the tower and the birds.

105

Perhaps this visionary dream is pointing out to us that the function of Obs₁ and Obs₂ is to educate Obs₃ in T₃. From the familiar viewpoint of body and mind all is changing, and this seems to serve no useful purpose. But there is a view from the

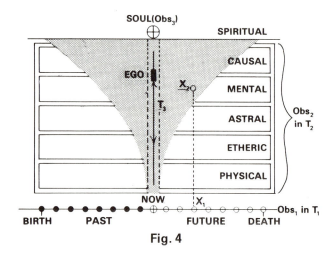

Fig. 4

tower by Obs₃ — the soul — and we shall all stand there some day as illuminated souls. In that moment we shall know that only God matters, and that nothing that could ever happen to us or which has happened, is of any account. As Priestley movingly says, of this view, 'It left nothing to mourn over behind it.'

Priestley's vision achieved the vision of Obs₃ in T₃ by the device of speeding T₂ up to such a degree that Obs₂ and Obs₃ could not follow it. The poet Rupert Brooke in his delightful poem *Dining Room Tea* achieved the view of Obs₃ by making T₂ stand still. I shall present part of it to you: he is describing a pleasant afternoon tea-party with a few friends that he loved. Then unheralded comes the immortal moment.

> Till suddenly, and otherwhence,
> I looked upon your innocence.
> For lifted clear and still and strange

106

From the dark woven flow of change
Under a vast and starless sky
I saw the immortal moment lie.
One instant I, an instant, knew
As God knows all. And it and you
I, above Time, Oh blind! could see
in witless immortality.
I saw the marble cup, the tea,
Hung on the air, an amber stream;
I saw the fire's unglittering gleam,
The painted flame, the frozen smoke.
No more the flooding lamplight broke
On flying eyes and lips and hair;
But lay, but slept unbroken there,
On stiller flesh, and body breathless,
And lips and laughter stayed deathless,
And words on which no silence grew.
Light was more alive than you.
For suddenly and otherwhence,
I looked on your magnificence.
I saw the stillness and the light,
And you, august, immortal, white,
Holy and strange; and every glint
Posture and jest and thought and tint
Freed from the mask of transiency,
Triumphant in eternity,
Immote, immortal.
Dazed at length
Human eyes grew, mortal strength
Wearied; Time began to creep.
Change closed about me like a sleep.
Light glinted on the eyes I loved.
The cup was filled. The bodies moved.
The drifting petal came to ground.
The laughter chimed its perfect round.
The broken syllable was ended.
And I, so certain and so friended,

How could I cloud, or how distress,
The heaven of your unconsciousness?
Or shake at Time's sufficient spell,
Stammering of lights unutterable?
The eternal holiness of you,
The timeless end, you never knew
The peace that lay, the light that shone.
You never knew that I had gone
A million miles away, and stayed
A million years. The laughter played
Unbroken round me; and the jest
Flashed on. And we that knew the best
Down wonderful hours grew happier yet.
I sang at heart, and talked, and ate,
And lived from laugh to laugh, I too,
When you were there and you and you.

Rupert Brooke, in his own perfect way, has told us that in the
moment when time stood still, he was able to look with his
soul's sight, and saw the one he loved

'Freed from the mask of transiency,
Triumphant in eternity,
Immote, immortal.'

He speaks of the eternal holiness of you. This was the soul of
his friend to which he felt related.

It is for the soul, a child of God, that time was created, that
she may enter when she is perfected through suffering, into
her eternally glorious inheritance in the Father's House.

Light of All Life –
An Appreciation of Mysticism

During past years, I have from time to time received letters from people who have told me of inner experiences which have come unexpectedly to them, which they could not account for, but which in general brought to them supersensible knowledge, and often had rich emotional overtones of peace, joy and bliss. Most of the writers said that these experiences were impossible to describe adequately in words, but they emphasized that they left behind them a legacy of certainty, as though for a short time a veil had been lifted revealing the presence of higher levels of consciousness. Such contact with higher levels of reality is what we call mystical experience. It cannot be commanded, although it can be prepared for. I came to feel through reading of these experiences and finally through first-hand experience, that here were to be found the answers to life's questing, for which all sincere souls are seeking, life after life. Since 1963, through the grace of a true Master, I have learned a great deal more of the mystic's path, and for this I am humbly and profoundly grateful.

First, let me clear away some misapprehensions. Mysticism has often been presented as the way of a questing soul, consciously separating herself from the life of the world, and orientated towards ascetic disciplines. There is of course a true element here: one cannot serve God and mammon. Indeed, one cannot have the best of both worlds, and a disciplined life is important if one seeks to progress along the path. The mystic has become aware of the underlying unity of all things, so he returns to the world to live and work *in* it, yet he is not *of* it. The mystic is aware of the existence of truth,

109

beauty, and knowledge far beyond levels to which the mind has access. He has come to know – not merely to believe – that there is a way home to the Father of all souls. The inner light of which he has become conscious, has been referred to by a poet as:

> The Light that never was on sea or land,
> The Consecration and the Poet's dream.

This light may shine from time to time within the inner sanctuary of the contemplative, but may shine also within the heart of the humble soul who cares enough for others to forget about himself.

The mystic's consciousness seems in such utter contrast with the age in which we live. True! This is why I am writing about it, so that we can remain balanced and trustful amid the uncertainty and insecurity of this age. The world is reaping the harvest of gross materialism, greed, and selfishness. We have cruelly exploited the animal kingdom for food. We have grown clever in the things of intellect and have become poverty-stricken in things of the spirit. The H-bomb is perhaps the most characteristic symbol of the world's present state.

The younger generation, appalled by the hypocrisy of many who are in power, are now seeking for life's meaning with an intensity perhaps never seen in any previous age. Remember that quite a proportion of them lost their lives in the Second World War, and are back again. Some have experienced higher levels of consciousness through mind-expanding drugs. Many have declined to participate in the rat-race of our civilisation, or fight wars which are thrust upon them by power-hungry politicians – although they are prepared to suffer in their own way for a better world. Some have intuited that the ancient tradition of India has preserved spiritual values which most of the Western tradition has ignored or thrown over. Hence their search for gurus and teachers of this older wisdom.

We do not need to go either to the East or the West for wisdom: it is within ourselves. I hope this chapter shows this

110

clearly. All souls long to get home to their Creator, but on the ego-level, few are conscious of this, and fewer still are prepared to sacrifice lesser pearls to find the pearl of great price. Our physical life is transient, and like our days at school, it is a preparation for so much more. It is offering to us, if we will only take the opportunity, the chance to learn certain lessons which we have to learn, and the opportunity to practise the great qualities of loving, caring, humility, courage, and trust in God.

Let us plunge into our subject. Evelyn Underhill defined mysticism as 'the art of union with reality'. She said, 'The mystic is a person who has attained that union in greater or lesser degree, or one who aims at that achievement.' Such definitions are perhaps less helpful than some practical examples. No two cases are alike, so I shall present three or four examples. The first from a young man of twenty:

'Suddenly in less than a second came this "feeling": a knowledge of oneness with ocean, sky, fish, birds, everything. The "feeling" was soon gone, but the impression remained ever since. It was not intellectual or emotional, but the feeling of certainty was there beyond all other feelings. I am surer of this than of anything else in life. It left a deep happiness which lasted for some hours. All was completely impersonal. "I was not there at all" is one way of expressing the "feeling". I have used the words oneness, happiness, certainty, and so on, but all are imperfect expressions – ludicrously so, of what I had experienced. At this time I had not read of mysticism, but later when I did, I was much interested to read of similar experiences. This experience left a mark on my intellectual life ever since.'

The second is part of a letter from a person I have not met:

'I cannot recall that I was thinking of anything in particular, when all of a sudden I was in a new dimension of experience. I can only attempt to explain this by saying that at one moment I was rigid, and the next I had become

111

fluid and merged with all there is. There was no sense of individual identity, yet personal awareness and appreciation remained. There was no past and no future, only awareness of living in an eternal moment that encompassed all that has been, that is, and that will be.

'I felt that I knew all, and nothing seemed to be unnecessary or out of place. There was perfect harmony and perfect blending of all into an indescribable expression of joy, peace, beauty, and love. One could only marvel and say "Of course! Of course!" It was all crystal-clear. One knew all in that moment, and yet knew nothing. I was contented and thankful beyond words just to experience *being*. The thought of God never crossed my mind, but immediately the experience passed I thought, "So that was God" or nirvana, or whatever word you use to express the inexpressible.

'During this experience I was aware of a veil just ahead of me, and within range of my finger-tips. I knew that if I reached out and parted the veil I would look upon the mystery of all life. An intense curiosity urged me to do this, but although I longed to look I could not bring myself to part the veil. I just felt that I could not look upon this awesome mystery. It was enough to know that it was there, and that all was well, now and always.

'Then, just as suddenly as I had found myself in the experience, I found myself back in the everyday world. It is a world little different from what it has always been, but for me there is one new dimension, and I don't think my world will ever contract back to its former limits . . . I suppose the end result of these experiences has been for me a realisation, despite all evidence to the contrary, that all is well now and always, that the power of love absorbs all and transcends all – and that the love of God is an ever-present reality – an ever-present reality that enfolds us always.'

This, the third account is taken from R. H. Ward's book *A Drug-Taker's Notes*. It is perhaps the most moving account of mystical experience which I have read anywhere.

I have meditated upon it, and know it is utterly true. Unfortunately there is only space to give you extracts. Mr Ward describes how it developed as he was walking home from the station. He describes the first signs as feeling like a 'rising-up within one self, or an inwardly coming alive'. He writes:

'I found I could think-and-feel in a new way. When I thought-and-felt about someone with whom I had been travelling on the train a few minutes before I understood him in a new way, which, while it was in no sense cold and uncaring was quite detached. To put it in one way, I knew him much better absent though he was, than I could ordinarily have done. Indeed many things which ordinarily I should not have been detached about, presented themselves as not mattering – as being quite unimportant. It was not that they were exactly trivial: they had simply got into their proper proportions. This caring and not-caring became a sort of theme of the experience as a whole; everything, whether things we attain in life or things we miss, is – I now understood – acceptable and right. This I realised was the real meaning of being at peace with the world. But it was not at all the same thing as disregarding the world, or being superior to it. It was accepting it. It was in a new, but very real sense, loving it.

'I noticed in regard to this thinking-and-feeling in a new way, that certain thoughts and feelings were dangerous. If I allowed any dislike, distrust, fear or contempt to approach, it had to be deliberately put away, or the rising up would begin to be a falling down.

'I had gone about a quarter of a mile and I found myself looking at an ugly little suburban villa, but now it appeared quite otherwise. I stood and stared at it and the mere sight of it filled me with joy . . . The house was changed, not so much in itself, but because I was looking at it with changed eyes . . . I realised that if one could always live on this level it would be another world in which

113

there would be nothing that we habitually call evil or ugly, and nothing which we habitually call good either, since the truth of these things is beyond these contradictions and somehow takes them up into itself.

'After this I began to look at everything around me. Time had little significance. Everything I saw was mysterious and wonderful . . . Things took on a new significance as with the house I had just passed, as though I had never seen it before. Even to pass from the shadow into the moonlight was an experience full of wonder. The trees by the wayside were incredible: they were incredibly more themselves than usual . . . I could somehow feel and understand the life of trees, yet always with that curious objectivity which increased rather than diminished my understanding of trees. They were different from me yet in no sense alien to me. I stood for a long time staring into the branches. I felt no identity with it, but I felt *it*. Indeed I adored it, and God for making it. The sheer joy I experienced in all this is beyond expression. I felt that the world of Nature was utterly right and literally an act of God's, and that to know this and to be permitted to appreciate so much of the wonderful and adorable was nothing less than bliss. *And this was reality*. That is the whole point . . .

'At one time it flashed upon me with irrefutable conviction "Of course there is God". It was an expression of the actual, real and immediate experience at that moment of God's existence. *God was here*. He was in everything I looked at and in me who looked. When I thought of certain people it was with a kind of passion of love for them which cherished their very existence, though still with detachment. One of these people was a friend who was dangerously ill with cancer. The strange certainty came to me that I could somehow make contact with her there and then, from this new state – that I could convey to her my own faith in the truth which involved the goodness and beauty of everything, and that this realisation would help her in her illness. For I understood that if she could be

114

where I was at that moment – in the presence of God – the neoplasms attacking her physical body could not be there . . . But at the same time I knew that it did not matter if this physical body of hers died. I had certainly never loved her as I did at this moment, yet for that very reason, death itself was unimportant, at least as far as I was concerned. Death was no more terrible than the reverse side of the coin of life. What we call life, the life of the knowledge of good and evil, which for a few minutes I had already escaped, was of no value compared with this different life in the presence of God, which death could in no real sense touch. I tried by a deliberate effort to feel my own life energy flowing towards my dying friend and strengthening her. In this different state of being one wants to give everything: it is what one exists to do.

'This new state fluctuated up and down. On one of the crests of renewed intensity, when the aperture of consciousness was at its widest, I heard vividly, shockingly, and as instantaneously as one might see a flash of lightning, what I can only call an inward voice which said *"There is something perfect"*. The voice seemed to be telling me in those four words, everything that it is important and necessary to know. "There is something perfect" was a summary of what it is to be in the presence of God, Who is perfection's Self. Since it is true that there is something perfect, all the imperfections to which we are heirs could be seen in their insignificant proportions. These words applied to my sick friend, to her self imprisoned in her sick body, to the trees and moonlit landscape even . . .

'I stood still in the road, filled to the brim with this wonderful and joyful realisation, that whatever we have to endure of pain, sickness, grief, and man's inhumanity to man, *there is still something perfect in all created things, that ultimately they live by it, and that nothing else matters*.

'Tears fell from my eyes. I had an impulse to go on my knees, there in the road beneath the stars which distantly

115

LIGHT OF ALL LIFE

gleamed through the rags of cloud, and yet were not distant at all, being bound with me, as I with them, in the sum of things under God's Hand . . . I knew very well I deserved nothing of what I had received, nothing whatever. It was pure grace. It was something for nothing which it is the nature of God to give to His prodigal sons.'

As I said at the beginning, I have meditated often upon this mystical experience, so sympathetically expressed, and I have deeply felt its insights and truth. One could multiply examples, but all of them depict certain characteristics; let me enumerate them.

Certainty – One mystic said, 'The feeling of certainty was there beyond all other feelings. I am surer of this than of anything else in my life.' In different words all of them use the strongest affirmation to express the reality and the irrefutable character of what came to them. Let us say here that the mind's knowledge is never certain: it embodies at most a high degree of probability. Only the soul's knowledge is certain.

Emotional Tones – All of them use such words as ecstasy, joy, bliss, love, beauty, and perfection. It is as though they are all vainly struggling to express the love they felt for everything, and which radiated from everything to them.

The Approach to One-ness or Unity – Perhaps this is the most significant element in mystical experience: it is this which separates it from psychical experience no matter what the level of consciousness. One mystic says, 'I felt one with all created things.' Another says, 'I saw there was no such thing as separateness, no such thing as the world apart from me.' Another says, 'I experienced in that moment a sense of profoundest kinship with each and every person there. I loved them all with a kind of love I had never felt before.' Another says, 'I became aware of a super-real state of being.' One felt one with it all and yet retained one's individuality. It is a paradox when expressed in words, but while being experienced no difficulty exists.

Insights into Truth – Some of the statements made after-

116

wards, are these: 'I knew beyond a shadow of doubt that at the heart of things was joy, beauty, and love.' 'All mankind is noble and loveable, only so mistaken and needlessly unhappy.' 'We have life within, compared with which the life of the body is but a shadow, and indeed of no value compared with the other.' 'I know that this life is only part of a whole, and that there are higher forms of consciousness.' 'We, our true selves, are not bounded by space and time.' 'Evil exists, but is restricted and controlled.'

Health of the Body – Not infrequently, those who have had mystical experience refer to the augmented health and vitality which followed. One young man told me how he had been out for a walk with his financee. They were climbing a hill, and she was troubled by severe asthmatic symptoms. I will quote his account.

'We struggled up the hill and the next thing I noticed was that the whole locality was illumined by an extraordinary bright light. It was a cloudy and dull day, and this extremely intense illumination did not appear to originate in any fixed centre, but was diffused equally throughout the entire locality. Accompanying the light was the sense of a presence of irresistible power, wholly and utterly benevolent, and as far as I was concerned a feeling of complete happiness and well-being, quite impossible to describe. The certainty of all-pervading and immutable love was so tremendous that I simply went on up the hill completely absorbed in this tremendous experience, and quite oblivious of the material surroundings. After an appreciable interval, I think a few minutes, the light gradually faded and I said to my companion, "Did you see that?" But she had noticed nothing unusual. However she turned to me and said, "My asthma has all gone", and this disease has never returned.'

Other cases could be quoted of spontaneous healing of the body arising through the mystical experience of a closely related soul. We recall Mr Ward's conviction about his friend dying of cancer, 'I understood that if she could be where I was at that moment – in the presence of God – the neoplasms attacking her physical body could not be there.' It is surprising how many of those who have had mystical experience use such a phrase as 'walking on air' to describe their elevation of spirit.

Appearance of Light – The presence of an unusual light is frequently mentioned by mystics. It is presumably subjective, since others in the vicinity are often quite unaware of anything. It is presumably the light of the spirit, which interpenetrates all levels from the physical upwards. This light is always shining within the lamp of the soul, but it is dimmed by the veils of the surrounding bodies.

I think enough has been said to give you an impression of what mystical experience is. In the second half of this chapter we must look at some of the questions which are asked about it, and we must interpret it and understand its importance for ourselves.

Let me begin by commenting that man's normal level of consciousness is a very restricted one, even though it is half way up the ladder of consciousness. At the bottom of the ladder we may place the consciousness of single cells both of the animal and vegetable kingdom. We would call this type *simple* consciousness. In the middle is man's type called self-consciousness. This is characterised by the existence of an ego-centre, which knows that it knows. At the top of the ladder is cosmic consciousness, which is of the soul – not the mind. Upon this no restrictions can be placed.

The self-consciousness of man, which is so restricted in time and space, leaves him asking innumerable questions, many beyond his power to answer. He sees man tossed like corks on the ocean of the opposites, between joy and sorrow, love and hate, peace and struggle, beauty and ugliness. He sees life as transient and change as constant, and asks, 'Is the universe friendly?' – or is it indifferent to our aspirations and hopes? When there is added to this picture man's selfishness,

118

greed, power-hunger, and indifference to his brother's welfare, is it any wonder that many people are asking, 'Is there any meaning in life? The world seems to have gone mad.'

In this situation it is reassuring to know that ordinary people like ourselves have had mystical glimpses, and are able to say to us, 'All is well. Don't be deceived by these appearances.' To quote Mr Ward again, he said: 'In a flash as it seemed to me, I saw the meaning – the meaning that is, of the universe, of life on earth, and of man . . . that everything is in order, that everything works according to an ineluctable pattern . . . Provided that we bear the pattern's existence in mind, even pain can have meaning, so can death, so can the worst that we may have to endure; while the possibility of discerning this meaning is itself the meaning of divine mercy.' Yes! the pattern is there for each individual life: accept it, trust it, and live at peace.

Many years ago I remember reading Vera Brittain's biography of Winifred Holtby, a brilliant Yorkshire novelist who died at the age of 37. She had been told by a London specialist about three years before, that she might have only a couple of years to live. Deteriorating health made a quiet country life necessary, but she felt rebellious against a fate that would cut short a life of service which her gifts and temperament well-qualified her to give. She was walking one day up a lonely road near Monks Risborough in a very dispirited frame of mind, and found herself approaching a drinking trough for the use of animals outside a farm house. It was a cold spring. The water in the trough was frozen over, and the lambs were trying in vain to drink. She broke the ice for them with her stick, and as she did so, she heard a voice within which seemed to say, 'Having nothing, yet possessing all things.'

She said later that this moment embodied the supreme spiritual experience of her life, and that from then on, all resentment, bitterness, and grief left her and did not return. She had made the same discovery as Mr Ward made when

119

walking along another road. I shall repeat his words, 'This caring and not-caring became a sort of theme of the experience as a whole; everything, whether things we attain in life, or things we miss, is – I now understood – acceptable and right. This I realised was the real meaning of being at peace with the world . . . it was accepting it.'

Winifred Holtby said that she always associated her experience with the words of Bosanquet the philosopher, who said,

'And now we are saved absolutely, we need not say from what; we are at home in the universe, and feeble and timid creatures as we are, there is nothing in the world or without it that can make us afraid.'

I want to look at the views of a sceptic who says, 'How do we know that the experience of these mystics is valid and trustworthy? They might be deluded or hallucinatory. We hear of mystical experiences taking place under anaesthetics, and under the influence of drugs such as L.S.D. or mescaline. Can these states of mind be trusted in the search for truth? As for the conviction and certainty expressed by some of those who have had them, there are persons who have delusions which they nevertheless hold with extreme tenacity.'

I reply that questions of 'proof' of the validity of experience are characteristic of the scientific method of approach. This is valid in its own field, but it is no ground for condemning other approaches such as are made by the historian, poet, artist, and philosopher. There are huge tracts of experience to which the scientific method is inapplicable. One area is that of our feelings. A person may say, 'I feel a pain' or 'I feel sad': he cannot prove this to another nor can anyone disprove his assertion. He alone knows what he feels. Our inward sensations are also of this character. They are private, except that we tend to assume that other people are like ourselves. But if you talked about the taste of a strawberry or the smell of a rose to a person without the senses of taste or smell, it would convey nothing to him.

Similarly, no one could convey what love is to a person who

had never experienced it. Likewise, we must not be unfair to the mystics who affirm what they have experienced with absolute conviction. There may be faculties awake in them which are not awake in us. We should rather recognise their claims and look for others who support their evidence. If we find that all down the ages persons of varying type and race, temperament and culture have reported similar things; it is far more likely that they have experienced truth than suffered from delusion.

A warning must be given however to the sceptic: mystical experience cannot be commanded by an act of will: it is an act of grace sometimes given to the soul that deserves it. It has however been a part of the great religious tradition that by purifying the self, following certain disciplines, and building a noble and unselfish character, the conditions are more likely to be favourable.

One must recognise that there are different approaches to truth. A scientist can say, 'Go into my laboratory and fulfil these conditions: you will see for yourself what happens.' He only asks for honesty. But in the search for spiritual knowledge the soul is involved – not the mind – so that the real observer is himself involved in the truth he is seeking. He is involved also as the instrument by which it is apprehended. In this rarefied air of truth's domain, we can only experience what we have fitted ourselves to experience by our love, trust, service and self-discipline. Pascal knew this when he wrote: 'Human things have to be known to be loved; divine things have to be loved to be known.'

To those who query mystical experience because in some cases drugs, fasting or other ascetic practices have been involved, I shall reply that these have no necessary connection, since there are many cases where no external factor is involved. But even if there were, it might be cogently argued that these outside factors are only triggers which stimulate the disclosure of what is already there. If we draw back a curtain from a window and this discloses a beautiful view, we do not claim that the removal of the curtain *created* the view, but rather that it disclosed what was there but unseen. It is the view that is important, and how much is seen when the curtain is drawn aside, depends upon the quality and soul-preparedness.

If we receive some important information, we are not very concerned whether it has come by post, private messenger, phone, telegram or radio. These have only been useful inter-mediate vehicles helping us to become aware of the know-ledge. That mystical knowledge has no necessary connection with delusional states is clear when we think of the quality of mind and life of some of the world's great mystics – Gautama the Buddha, Lao-Tze, Mo-Ti, Kabir, Nanak, Plotinus, Dante, Sufis like Jellal-ad-din-Rumi, Ruysbroek, Eckhart, Boehme, Edward Carpenter, etc.

Note also the unexpectedness of the timeless moment, and the passivity of the experiencer in the presence of power and glory far beyond his normal experience. Note also the uplift-ment, courage, inspiration, and utter gratitude which mystics have felt for what has been shown to them. One of them said, 'I realised that in that half-hour under ether, I had served God more distinctly and purely than I had ever done in my life before.' Dr R. M. Bucke, a distinguished Canadian psy-chiatrist had an illuminative experience and said of it after-wards, 'It was impossible for me ever to forget what at that time I saw and knew, neither did I, nor could I ever doubt the truth of what was then presented to my mind.' I shall say no more in defence of mysticism, but quote the words of a great Master who said, 'He that hath ears to hear, let him hear.'

I come now to a faltering and humble attempt to try to interpret what is happening in mystical experience. The sug-gestions I make are only to be thought of as a groping towards truth. As one reads the accounts of mystical experi-ence it is not easy to classify them. One can see that some touch higher levels of consciousness than others. The levels of reality are like a ladder up which the consciousness may be lifted. Let me present an account which I would regard as borderline between what we call psychical and the mystical.

One day when I was playing golf, my companion lost a ball. As I searched for it I stood beside a young wattle tree coming into bloom. I gazed at it quite delighted, giving it my whole attention. Then an indescribable thing happened. As I stared at it, its beauty grew until it was transformed into a living glowing pitch of intensity past all imagining. It remained so for at least thirty seconds, during which I could have gone on seeing it in its transformed state, had I been able to sustain it, i.e. to maintain some sort of focus.

It seems likely that consciousness was lifted to the astral level, so that this might be called a type of clairvoyance – the light on that level being far brighter. Let me take one further example which could be classed as nature-mysticism. This goes much higher in consciousness. I have only space to include a small part of this account obtained from my deceased friend Ambrose Pratt, through the mediumship of the late Geraldine Cummins. My friend describes how he had been preparing himself to appreciate the unitive principle behind nature as it appeared on a small island in the Gulf of Mexico. He describes it first as seen on the etheric level, and then he lifts consciousness to probably the Causal level. I now quote him:

'I had the sensuous human pleasure of perceiving it all. But how trivial was that pleasure when my mind gradually went inward to genie. The process might be likened to that of a seagull on a cliff with shut wings, just before its take-off from a jutting rock. Suddenly the great wings are outspread and it is off, rising, soaring above the immensities of the ocean beneath the wide cirrus-streaked skies. It is a poor simile, but how except objectively can I convey to you the ecstasy of that flight into union. Then I knew the unity behind the separate myriad forms animated by life on that small island. I was one with the divine imagining actively maintaining and conserving that fragment of nature. I was one with the Artist experiencing the creative rapture which was His; one with the essence, the conception, containing as well the physical representation. I was aware of the large, the little, the infinitesimal on that island. I experienced breath of life animating the tiniest coloured insect there. But it came like a chorus, many voices making one earth-time song. There is a quotation from the gospels which I then truly apprehended, "One sparrow shall not fall without your heavenly Father knowing it."'

I shall not quote any further from this remarkable account – which came, as I said, from the 'other side of life'. To me it seems that he may have lifted his consciousness to the Causal level from which there come the greatest creative inspirations of all art. Indeed, may I quote one more sentence. He wrote of this level, 'The initiatory conception is a country where beauty has no ebb, no decay, no rotting, no withering – where joy is wisdom, and time an endless melody.'

It was said by Mozart's biographer that he was able to apprehend and appreciate some of his musical works *as a whole*, i.e. to know them totally, before he expended the necessary energy to spread them out in time. This would be essentially high mystical knowledge, such as those of you who followed the last chapter would describe as knowledge of Obs_3 in T_3. Now I would like you to look at another diagram which has been constructed to illustrate certain relationships on the spiritual level. I hope it will not be taken too seriously – but I often feel that a diagram can help us sometimes as much as, if not better than words. When the sense of unity becomes marked, it is often interpreted by the mystic as awareness of the divine presence. In one sense this is true: but it is only in a minor sense – for the presence of the eternal spirit flows downwards through all levels and may be apprehended on any level with consciousness on a higher level. The radiation of the sun is felt throughout the solar system, but this is not the same as a full contact with the sun. I suggest that the majority of high mystical experiences involve the lifting of consciousness towards the soul-level.

The soul's viewpoint is then described as well as may be, by the mystic. If consciousness is lifted any higher I think it is an awareness or communion of that soul with the spirit of the soul-group to which it belongs. (Stage 1 of diagram.) This is as far as man can go while incarnate. It may be this stage, which when completed is known as Illumination or the Beatific Vision or Nirvikalpa Samadhi. From this state the consciousness falls back again nearer to the normal type, but it is for ever changed by this experience, and describes it as direct knowledge of God. (You recall Mr Ward's magnificent description.) I will try in a few sentences to say something about the soul-groups.

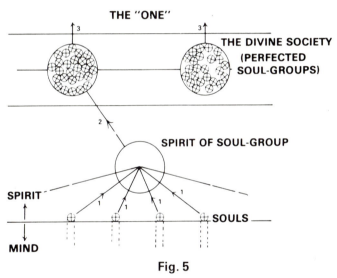

Fig. 5

A soul-group may contain a score or perhaps a thousand souls, who are all nourished by one and the same spirit. It is a finite but great divine being, individualised by God in the sense that 'it has the apartness of the created thing from the source which gave it birth'. A group of souls probably shares a common collective unconscious mind as well as being nourished by the one spirit. When an individual soul becomes directly aware of its parent source, this is easily interpreted as

125

union with God. This spirit grows and unfolds through the growth and maturing of its individual souls. When these souls have all reached Illumination, then the soul-group may as a whole make transit to a still higher lever, where it will discover its relationship to other completed soul-groups. I have called this level the divine society.

On this level it may proceed to gather experience of other galaxies than our own. It is of no value to speculate further, but undoubtedly there are higher states of consciousness (represented by 2 and 3 in the diagram), and there may be no end to the spiritual journey. To suppose that there is an 'end' is failure to recognise those attributes of eternity and infinity which pertain to the light of the supreme spirit. My old friend Ambrose Pratt wrote to me through the mediumship of Geraldine Cummins as follows:

> 'I should like to write a cautionary tale for the mystics who still occupy the confined cell of the physical body, though now and then they briefly experience what some describe as union with God. Here is my cautionary tale.
>
> ' "Jupiter fell in love with Semele, and he revealed himself to her as a man. She thought herself strong enough to meet him on her own level – to be loved by a god. So she demanded insolently that he should come to her in his full divine status. What happened? She withered away – consumed by his fire.''
>
> 'Too considerable a revelation of God would drive the most spiritual human being mad. The highly gifted mystic or yogi was never in his earthly life-time linked with God. Actually his little spark was blown upon so that it became a tiny flame during the occasions when he had mystical experience. Only when the long journey through infinite time has been made, only when the human soul has been fully used for purposes of the divine imagination, and when this soul is incomparably enriched by the strength of all the other souls in its group, can it experience union with divine imagination. To be on a level with God one has to become a god, and that full glory is not to be experienced by any human being.'

126

Surely this is true. Now let us return from these heights to our familiar life before we close. The world of clashing opposites in which we live our lives is only partially real; the Indians call it *maya*. By *maya* they mean the delusion of ignorance. The primary ignorance – the densest of the veils which the mind imposes on us, leads us to identify ourselves with our ego. So we remain ignorant of our true self, just as a dreamer does of his waking self when he continues to dream. But just as in dreams some fragments and symbols arise which are echoes of our waking life, so we hear at times in our waking life echoes and whispers of something that we greatly yearn for but cannot understand. This quest for true and permanent happiness lures us on. It is the call of the soul to be recognised as the true self and known. But men do not know this and they look outside and plunge into the world of the opposites to find it. Craving and desire are expressions of the ego's search for happiness – where it can never be found.

What then is the truth about this troubled, storm-tossed world into which we have been born and have to live our lives? It has some beauty as all the poets and artists have felt, but it is nevertheless the lowest and darkest of all the levels of partial reality. Compared with it, the astral levels to which we shall pass at death are idyllic, peaceful and secure. Mystics who have lifted their consciousness even to the mind levels have told us of things in marked contrast with their ordinary view – and they were convinced of the truth they perceived.

'Love pervades everything, sustains it and undergirds it. All conflict and suffering are like surface waves upon the quiet ocean depths.

'There is a great unity of structure and purpose which they have glimpsed. In spite of all apparent contradictions, they have glimpsed the divine purpose working onwards to a perfect goal. One mystic said, "I often doubted before, but I never doubted after this." Tagore said eloquently, "Our life, like a river, strikes its banks, not to feel shut in by them, but to realise anew every moment that it has its unending opening towards the sea."

127

'Finally, "Of course there is God". I repeat this sentence because it expresses the foundation truth of all mystical experience. As Mr Ward said, "There is something perfect in all created things; ultimately they live by it – and nothing else matters." '

To realise this is to know the light of all life. We must express it in our living. It can be done by serving others cheerfully in humble and menial tasks, by showing courage and serenity when suffering, by bringing beauty into drab surroundings, and by bringing peace to those who are fearful. 'Blessed are the peacemakers for they shall be called the children of God.'